GWR STATIONS

COTSWOLDS AND SOUTHWEST ENGLAND

GWR STATIONS

COTSWOLDS AND SOUTHWEST ENGLAND

ALLEN JACKSON

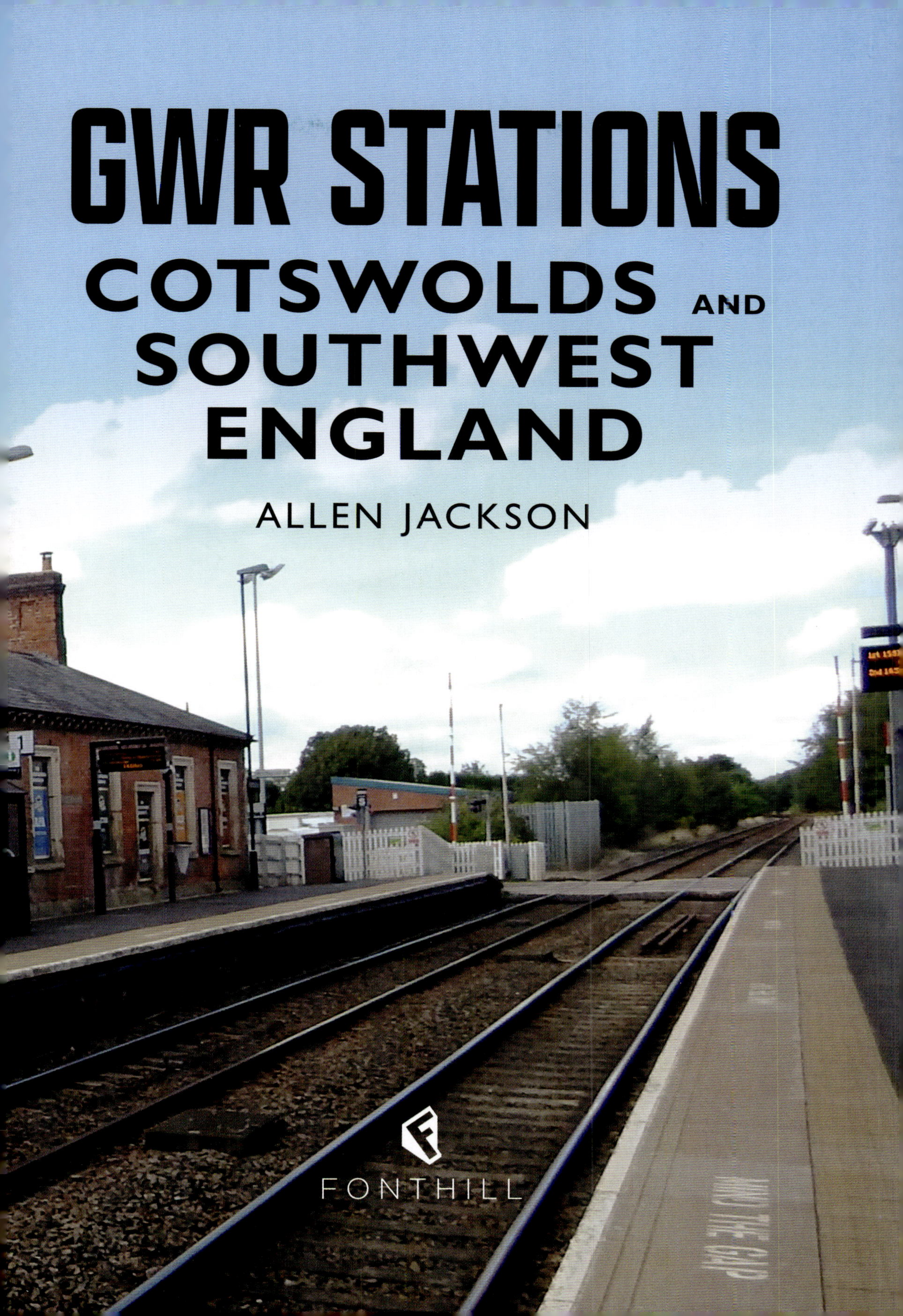

FONTHILL

First published in Great Britain in 2026 by
Fonthill
An imprint of
Pen & Sword Books Ltd
Yorkshire – Philadelphia

ISBN 978-1-03614-732-7

A CIP catalogue record for this book is available from the British Library.

Typeset in SabonLTStd 10/13 by
SJmagic DESIGN SERVICES, India.
Printed and bound in India by Replika Press Pvt Ltd

MIX
Paper | Supporting responsible forestry
FSC™ C016779

The Publisher's authorised representative in the EU for product
safety is Authorised Rep Compliance Ltd., Ground Floor,
71 Lower Baggot Street, Dublin D02 P593, Ireland.
www.arccompliance.com

For a complete list of Pen & Sword titles please contact

PEN & SWORD BOOKS LIMITED
George House, Units 12 & 13, Beevor Street, Off Pontefract Road,
Barnsley, South Yorkshire, S71 1HN, England
E-mail: enquiries@pen-and-sword.co.uk
Website: www.pen-and-sword.co.uk

or

PEN AND SWORD BOOKS
1950 Lawrence Rd, Havertown, PA 19083, USA
E-mail: uspen-and-sword@casematepublishers.com
Website: www.penandswordbooks.com

Contents

The Tudoresque splendour of Shrewsbury was in part due to its being a joint station with the LNWR (LMS).

Introduction

In 2013, through my observations of rail developments then in progress, it could be seen that much of the Great Western glory of architecture, some of it in quite small stations, would be changed by disabled access, modernisation and electrification—as indeed much of it subsequently has been. This book presents a view of the recent past where the accent is the stations themselves rather than a train that just happens to be there. Some views are of signal boxes only, as that is all that has survived at a particular location, but these too are time limited in operation.

This book is about the railway company that existed from 1835 to 1947, albeit in a modern context. The rebranding of the Train Operating Company (TOC) First Great Western to Great Western Railway inevitably features from time to time, as it is their trains in some of the photographs. Where this is the case, the TOC will be designated to avoid confusion. Some stations were absorbed by the grouping of 1923 but have been subsumed under the GWR banner.

The Berks and Hants line was most definitely a GWR main line, but the rest of the area covered is devoted to secondary routes that lacked the glamour of the holiday lines. Yet modernisation has passed them by to some extent, and so they retain much more of the character and flavour of the old company than elsewhere.

Isambard Kingdom Brunel is forever associated with the Great Western and some of the designs were attributed to him, although there were many assistants and pupils who may have done the drawings and been involved on a day-to-day basis.

The book is arranged in terms of journeys, and diagrams of the routes are included.

Listed buildings

Many GWR structures are considered to have architectural and historic merit and are either Grade I or Grade II listed by Historic England or Historic Wales (CADW). Both Grade I and II buildings require permission to make exterior or interior alterations. However, Grade II listings, which are by far the most common, generally enjoy more leeway, particularly with the interior. If a building has been left to decay to such an extent that it becomes unsafe, permission may be granted for demolition.

Summary of Contents

The territory covered does not include the Great Western Main Line from Paddington to Bristol and then on to Penzance, which has been covered in a previous volume.

Some stations names have been modified, usually shortened, in recent years but the old GWR names have been used, which were usually derived from the name on the original act of parliament for the line. This means that grammar and spelling are not always what would usually be regarded as correct. In addition, Welsh stations were usually reduced to some form of Anglicisation. Dates given for each station table indicate the date of the current structure, where known, not the date of the construction of the original line, although there are a few buildings where the two dates are one and the same.

Berkshire–Hampshire–Wiltshire–Dorset–Somerset

Cotswolds, Worcester and Hereford

Worcester Foregate Street
Malvern Link
Great Malvern
Ledbury
Hereford Barrs Court

Wolverhampton to Chester

Codsall
Albrighton
Cosford
Shifnal
Oakengates
Wellington
Shrewsbury (Joint station with the LNWR/LMS)
Baschurch
Gobowen
Ruabon
Wrexham General
Chester General (Joint station with the LNWR/LMS)

Worcestershire

Droitwich Spa
Hartlebury
Kidderminster
Churchill and Blakedown
Hagley
Stourbridge Junction

Gloucestershire

Kemble
St Mary's Crossing
Stroud
Gloucester Central
Lydney

Severn Beach Line

Montpelier
Redwood
Clifton Down
Sea Mills
Shirehampton
Avonmouth
St Andrews Road

The GWR took the time and trouble to embellish the humble footbridge with this confident decoration at Codsall.

1

Berkshire–Hampshire–Wiltshire–Dorset–Somerset

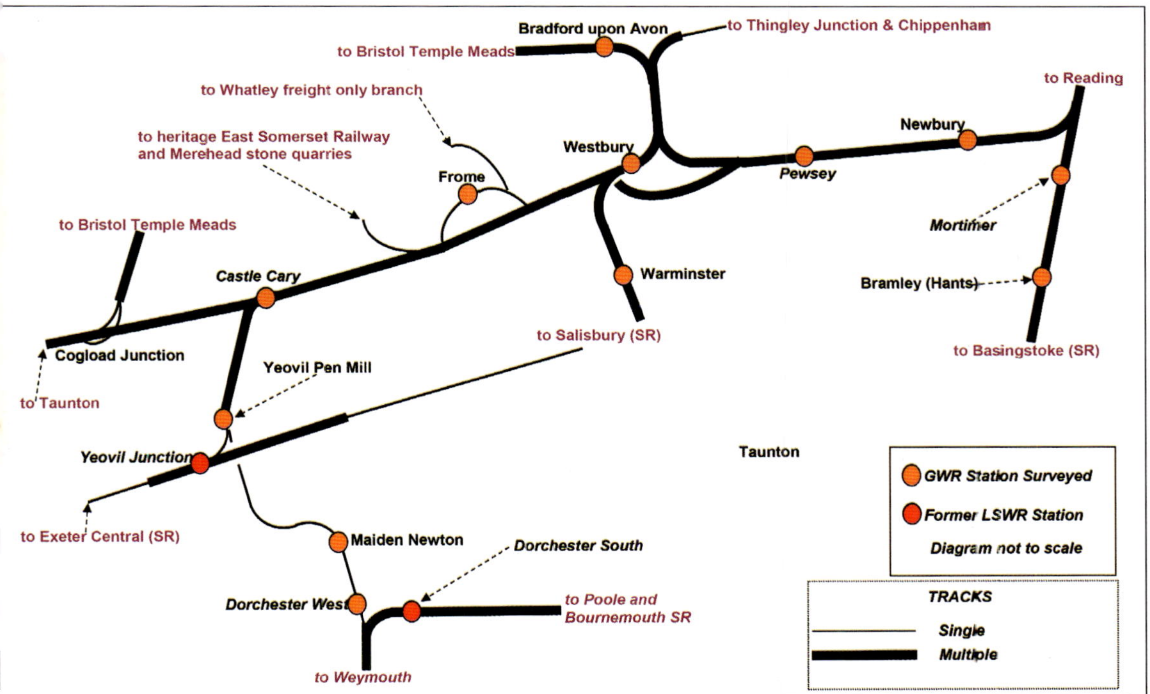

Figure 1. The diagram of the southwest counties is representative of the Network Rail situation in 2016. The GWR had their own stations at Basingstoke and Salisbury but the trains now run to former LSWR (SR) structures. The journey starts south of Reading at Brunel's Mortimer.

Mortimer

Date Built	Railway/Design	Platforms	Passengers 2023–2024	Listed
1848	GWR/Isambard Kingdom Brunel (IKB)	2	0.138 million	Grade II

Reading station nearby is now the acme of modernity but here, a few miles away, time has stood still somewhat. Mortimer was designed by Brunel in the then-fashionable Italianate style, which vied with the French style for architectural attractiveness, as can be seen at Slough in a previous volume. Chepstow exhibits some of the features and is covered in the companion volume to this one.

Above: **Figure 2.** The view north from the footbridge towards Reading depicts an almost unaltered Brunel station in the Italianate style. However, the pantile roofs are a product of the recent (1980s) restoration, which replaced GWR later-applied Welsh slates. May 2013.

Opposite above: **Figure 3.** The Historic England listing has this to say: 'Railway Station. 1848 by I K Brunel for the GWR. Red brick with stock brick strings and surrounds to openings; hipped slate roof with deeply projecting eaves on cut brackets. Single storey.' Clearly, Historic England is describing the building before its restoration. May 2013.

Opposite below: **Figure 4.** Although the waiting shelter was only ever thus, it retains the patterned brickwork to suggest the presence of windows. The platform seat has the GWR Art Deco monogram dating from 1934. May 2013.

Mortimer station is 43 miles and 14 chains (66.85km) from Paddington.

Bramley (Hampshire)

Date Built	Railway/Design	Platforms	Passengers 2023–2024	Listed
1895	GWR	2	0.241 million	No

This building resembles the model Airfix Construction Kit, except for the canopy, that was on sale for 10p or two shillings in the 1960s and, in common with many other property prices, has risen sharply. The GWR still managed to make attractive structures as time went on and budgets tightened up.

Above: **Figure 5.** Class 165, 165121 waits for passengers at Bramley to go forward to Basingstoke where some of the sidings there are still known as 'Great Western Sidings'. May 2013.

Opposite above: **Figure 6.** The standard GWR small station building of the late nineteenth century is shown here at Bramley. Spear fencing and corrugated iron shed work, both popular but un-trumpeted GWR architectural features, are in attendance. Spear fencing was said to be produced from old locomotive boiler tubes and sent out from Swindon as ready-built kit modules with right-angle stands. May 2013.

Opposite below: **Figure 7.** The waiting shelter on platform 2 at Bramley has decorative blue bricks and a chimney stack. May 2013.

Bramley station is 46 miles and 41 chains (71.64km) from Paddington.

Newbury

Date Built	Railway/Design	Platforms	Passengers 2023–2024	Listed
1910 Rebuilt	GWR	3	1.38 million	No

The 1910 rebuild was a statement piece of the importance of a junction of two branch lines. The Didcot, Newbury and Southampton Railway and the Lambourn Branch were the two lines running in. Kemble is a further example but on a lesser scale and was built earlier. The importance and overall impression of the station is heightened by the four tracks running through it.

Figure 8. The Edwardian era modernisation at Newbury produced this subsidiary building on platform 1. March 2007.

Figure 9. The main building on platform 1 at Newbury is impressive, with a massive connection to the footbridge. September 2016.

Figure 10. Platform 3, the bay, is still known as the Compton Bay, after a station on the long-closed Didcot Newbury and Southampton (DN&S) branch line. The bay is currently used for services to Reading. September 2016.

Figure 11. Further west, the locations of two more bay platforms are revealed, the further for the Lambourn branch and the nearer for the DN&S branch southwards. The main platforms are serviced by long loops from the double track main line. The view is east towards Reading. March 2007.

Newbury station is 53 miles and 6 chains (85.42km) from Paddington.

Pewsey

Date Built	Railway/Design	Platforms	Passengers 2023–2024	Listed
1862 Main building	Berks and Hants Railway	2	0.187 million	No

Pewsey was originally on a branch line, but the 1906 Castle Cary cut-off witnessed most of the GWR West of England expresses thunder through at high speed. Trevor Beaven served at Pewsey for over 50 years, much of it as stationmaster, and received the MBE for his work in 1999. He was not unique in post and the stationmaster at Twyford, Norman Topson, served for over 50 years at the one station. The GWR had many loyal servants and these men were their successors.

Above: **Figure 12.** The Berks and Hants line moves on to Wiltshire and survives as double track beyond Newbury, perhaps partly because of the stone and aggregate traffic from Merehead in Somerset. The station building on the down platform on the right at Pewsey is a modern reproduction. August 2016.

Opposite above: **Figure 13.** The reproduction waiting shelter looks completely at home with older platform seats, replica, early years twentieth-century-style running in board and sloping shelter. Mr Trevor Beaven MBE revealed that the footbridge there then had come from Cookham in Berkshire (since replaced), and the platform seats from the depot at Exeter Riverside. August 2016.

Opposite below: **Figure 14.** The beautifully kept waiting room, with GWR map, replica posters and some furniture, was part of Trevor's domain at this award-winning station. August 2016.

Pewsey station is 75 miles and 26 chains (121.22km) from Paddington.

Westbury (Wiltshire)

Date Built	Railway/Design	Platforms	Passengers 2023–2024	Listed
1901 Rebuilt	GWR	3	0.535 million	No

Westbury station was also rebuilt as the GWR traffic outgrew its original facilities. As a considerable junction, Westbury was a slip coach destination for Weymouth, where GWR coach or coaches would be detached from a train at speed and brought to a stand in the station, or just outside it, for onward transmission. There was a sizeable loco depot here too, modernised by Churchward. Westbury still sees considerable freight train activity, mainly centred on aggregate and ballast traffic.

Figure 15. The four platforms at Westbury have been reduced to three, where the fourth platform on the far left has surrendered its running line to the Down Reception siding at this busy freight location. The loop is currently holding two freight trains, which in GWR days would have been worked under 'permissive block' arrangements, quite common then but rare in the twenty-first century. The main station building is off to the left at the lower street level. August 2016.

Figure 16. Westbury station building and the DB Schencker branded class 59, 59204 is the same one we saw on the left in the previous figure. August 2016.

Figure 17. The other end of Westbury station looking back towards Pewsey. The iron columns holding up the roof date from 1899. The class 150 in platform 2 is headed for Castle Cary and the first of the two freights on the right has edged forwards to allow the second with the class 59 to nudge up also, thus avoiding the wagons fouling the running lines. August 2016.

Figure 18. On the far left the first of the two freights, class 66 hauled, edges up to the colour light signal, which is still 'on' or at danger. The green feathered colour light 'off' signal is set for Warminster and Salisbury. The yards on the right consist of DB Cargo sidings with the cement train and class 66, 66003 shunting aggregate wagons, with, on the far right, a Network Rail virtual quarry with at least a couple of Colas Rail class 70s. August 2016.

Westbury station is 109 miles and 64 chains (176.38km) from Paddington.

Bradford-on-Avon

Date Built	Railway/Design	Platforms	Passengers 2023–2024	Listed
1848	Wiltshire, Somerset and Weymouth	2	0.486 million	Grade II

Bradford-on-Avon is another attractive Brunellian icon that has survived where others, just as worthy, perished mainly in the 1960s and 1970s closure and cost cutting exercises. Where there was local pressure things would often remain as they were, in addition functional buildings would often not be as valued as others.

Figure 19. Many of Brunel's early stations were in timber, but the use of Bath stone means the station fits in with much else of the delightful Bradford-on-Avon, which is a kind of mini-Bath although not as ancient. June 2012.

Figure 20. The waiting shelter on the south side at Bradford-on-Avon station is no less grand in its way, but note how the early twentieth-century canopy was configured to network with the original footbridge, now no longer with us. It was unusual to provide such fitting and commodious secondary buildings on a way-side station. The replica name board up the platform does not have parliamentary hyphenation. June 2012.

Figure 21. The view of the north platform building at Bradford-on-Avon is from the car park. See how the platform canopy is continued around the sides. Also, there is parliamentary railway hyphenation in the name. June 2012.

Bradford-on-Avon station is 7 miles and 9 chains (11.45km) from Bathampton Junction with the GWR main line towards Bath.

Warminster

Date Built	Railway/Design	Platforms	Passengers 2023–2024	Listed
1851	Wiltshire, Somerset and Weymouth	2	0.331 million	No

Warminster station retains many original features, including wooden platform structures, although the canopies are a 1930s alteration. There is also a later substantial stationmaster's house, similar to that illustrated at Culham. It was as well that these houses were comfortable, as the stationmaster was expected to be almost permanently on duty or available.

Above: **Figure 22.** The view from the footbridge at Warminster reveals two wooden station buildings of some age, although the canopies and roofing are later. Note how even the small waiting room on the down side towards Salisbury has a fireplace. The trailing crossover allows any train to reverse direction as though it terminates here. August 2016.

Opposite above: **Figure 23.** Although not listed, the Warminster main station building is in remarkable condition for a timber building more than 160 years old. There had been an overall roof until the 1930s, whence the roof was replaced by canopies. The goods yard was to the right of the camera, and the stationmaster's house to the left and behind slightly. Observe the canopy valancing applied purely as decoration and the cranked drain pipe ventilator reminiscent of the contrived brake van in *The Titfield Thunderbolt* film (1953), although this one doesn't appear to pivot in the middle. August 2016.

Opposite below: **Figure 24.** Southwest Trains class 158, 158955 departs for Westbury. The buffet on the platform, just about where the last vehicle is, was a welcome refreshment. August 2016.

Warminster station is 114 miles and 37 chains (184.21km) from Paddington.

Frome

Date Built	Railway/Design	Platforms	Passengers 2023–2024	Listed
1850	Wiltshire, Somerset and Weymouth Hannaford	1 in use	0.169 million	Grade II

Hannaford, the architect, was a pupil of Brunel and this rare timber train shed reflects his style. Once again, a station that echoes the delightful nature of the town to which it belongs. As the station was also a junction with lines to Castle Cary, Bristol and Westbury, the freight facilities were extensive with a single-track engine shed, and there were three signal boxes here. Frome was bypassed in the 1930s with government/taxpayer assistance from the 1929 Loans Guarantees and Grants Act, and the West of England expresses no longer call here. The speed limit through the station is 35mph and on the cut off the line the maximum speed was 70mph.

Above: **Figure 25.** J.R. Hannaford's train shed and station buildings at Frome survive almost intact and are now listed and well cared for. As with Warminster, light and dark stone are back as GWR structure colours. This is the only survivor of a Brunel timber train shed at a through station. August 2016.

Opposite above: **Figure 26.** The line has been single track through here since BR days and the line was bypassed with the present loop in 1933 to avoid the station as a bottleneck. The replica running in board sits well with Brunel's design, complete with spear fencing. August 2016.

Opposite below: **Figure 27.** The wrought iron tie rods, picked out in black, emphasise the complexity of the overall roof. The platform seats appear to have replica timbers but original cast iron ends. The platforms themselves have been cut back to two-car DMU length and there had been a canopy on the left-hand platform after the train shed. August 2016.

Frome station is 115 miles and 44 chains (185.96km) from Paddington.

Castle Cary

Date Built	Railway/Design	Platforms	Passengers 2023–2024	Listed
1856	Wiltshire, Somerset and Weymouth R.P. Brereton	3	0.309 million	No

Castle Cary remains a junction with the Weymouth line but is now well known as the rail hub for Glastonbury Festival. The station junction received attention from the Luftwaffe in the Second World War, and the now-demolished signal box was a casualty but the goods shed and station building escaped. The signal box was replaced with an ARP-style building in 1942, but that too has not survived from a different kind of attack.

Figure 28. Most of what remains at Castle Cary is on view here. In the far distance, the road over the main line is just behind the goods shed, whose yard is the car park. The view is towards Taunton. Platform 3 services the branch to Yeovil and Weymouth, which is now single track. In signalling terms, the Weymouth line was originally regarded as the main line, no doubt as a result of its Wiltshire, Somerset and Weymouth Railway origins. The point in the foreground on the branch is to a pair of looped sidings, which would enable a locomotive to arrive at the head of train in one direction and then set off, still at the head of the train, in another direction. As most traffic is DMU or HST centred, the sidings would appear disused. August 2016.

Figure 29. A closer look at Castle Cary's canopy is greatly assisted by the supporting ironwork contrasting strongly with the rest of the structure. The canopy was cut back in later years. GWR shirt button monogram seats are in use and the former 'Gents' has the privacy screen in place. August 2016.

Figure 30. The super-elevation of the track shows up here as a westbound HST pulls into platform 2. Some cant is needed here, as the speed limit at the other end of the platform is 100mph (160km/h). The station has won awards in the 'best kept' category. August 2016.

Figure 31. The end of platform 2 is just on the left, controlled by Westbury's signal number 156. The feather allows trains to join the Weymouth branch from platform 2 and this would be needed if an HST were the motive power, as platform 3 can only handle a couple of coaches. The point on the right is to an engineer's siding. There is no crossover at this end of the station here to enable Weymouth trains to access the up platform 1 for Paddington. August 2016.

Castle Cary station is 129 miles and 45 chains (208.51km) from Paddington via Swindon, and 115 miles and 32 chains (185.72km) from Paddington via the Berks and Hants line and Westbury.

Yeovil Pen Mill

Date Built	Railway/Design	Platforms	Passengers 2023–2024	Listed
1854	Wiltshire, Somerset and Weymouth	3 faces 2 tracks	0.166 million	No

Yeovil Pen Mill has survived whilst the larger GWR/Southern Railway Town joint station has not, but the single track to SR Yeovil Junction station remains. Also, the semaphore signalling is still there, although, after 60 years under SR control, Southern Region signals exist with Western Region examples, as well as a GWR signal box.

Figure 32. Yeovil Pen Mill is the first and last station on the route with an active signal box and semaphore signals. The bracket signals control either the single track onwards to Dorchester on the right or the line that joins the former LSWR route at Yeovil Junction on the left. Although this station had been part of the Southern region since the 1960s, only in the 2000s have the GWR signal arms been replaced by Southern Region pattern ones, although some GWR pattern signals remain here.

The goods loops and long siding on the right are only used for permanent way purposes now. The exit from the loop is protected by a lower-quadrant ground signal and a double-railed trap point. Note the manual point lever without GWR guard rail. Each bracket signal has a notice reminding the driver to obtain the single line token before proceeding towards the camera. March 2009.

Figure 33. The main station building at Yeovil Pen Mill is a substantial structure built of local stone. The attractive colouration is said to be caused by the amount of iron oxide in the material. March 2009.

Figure 34. Some of the railway side of Yeovil Pen Mill station is rendered and this view shows the unique arrangement of the footbridge. Note that each platform face is separately numbered whereas there are only two tracks. Trains to Weymouth use platform 3. March 2009.

Figure 35. The GWR signal box controls the layout here, and both single lines south use 110-year-old key token apparatus where a physical token is issued to the train driver. The tracks behind the box are from near to far: platform 3, loop running line, loops run round and long siding. See there is a GWR pattern lower-quadrant signal past the box. August 2016.

Yeovil Pen Mill station is 141 miles and 27 chains (227.46km) from Paddington via Swindon.

Maiden Newton

Date Built	Railway/Design	Platforms	Passengers 2023–2024	Listed
1857	Wiltshire, Somerset and Weymouth R.P. Brereton	2	21,672	Grade II

There was some degree of standardisation on the Westbury to Salisbury and Westbury to Weymouth sections, and this station remains an example of the genre, albeit with peculiarities of its own. The now single-track main line to Weymouth is provided with a passing place here. Maiden Newton was the junction for the Bridport branch and had a bay platform, with overall roof, to service those branch trains. The line was latterly handed over to the Southern Region, and evidence of this is the possibly Exmouth Junction Southern Region manufactured concrete footbridge.

Above: **Figure 36.** The station buildings and footbridge are listed here and Maiden Newton is a passing place. It was the junction for the Bridport branch until 1975 and signs of the branch exist, as well as informative story boards detailing the branch working in steam days. There was a small overall roof over the branch bay platform in steam days. November 2007.

Opposite above: **Figure 37.** The signal box at the end of platform 2 is also listed but closed and dates from 1921. There had been an engineer's siding after platform 1 end on the right, but all that was left in 2016 was a pair of buffer stops. August 2016.

Opposite below: **Figure 38.** The signal box interfaced to Yeovil Pen Mill for the single line key token working. From Maiden Newton onwards, the line is worked Tokenless Block, which was invented by the Western Region of BR in the 1960s to speed up single line working. Although the signal box has been closed since 1988, special arrangements are in place for these two different methods of single line working. Observe that there is bullhead keyed track with two-bolt chair fixing and some chairs are marked GWR. August 2016.

MAIDEN NEWTON

HST
STOP
HST
Stop
Look
Listen

Figure 39. In this view towards Yeovil, the two grey cabinets at the far end of platform 1 and the near end of platform 2 both house single-line apparatus. The platform 1 box houses the token apparatus for the train driver to remove a token for Yeovil and the 'train arrived' switch, to convey to Dorchester South signal box that the train has completed the journey over the Tokenless Block section from Dorchester. The platform 2 box also has a token apparatus to enable the train driver to surrender the Yeovil Pen Mill section token and advise Dorchester that the train is ready to enter the Tokenless Block section. The up-running line is on the left and the direction of travel is away from the camera. This means that the point in the foreground is a catch point, meant to derail a runaway vehicle travelling in the opposite direction to normal. However, it is clamped out of use. The BR Southern Region concrete footbridge is also listed, but in far worse condition than the much older GWR structures. August 2016.

Figure 40. The BR Southern Region footbridge has breeze blocks holding up one side on the left. The Bridport bay and overall roof were on the right by the grey fencing. Because of a lack of space for a run round loop, the arriving tank engine (typically 45XX or 57XX) would pull into the bay, then reverse up an inclined siding, uncouple and switch to the branch track and the allow the coaches, latterly a GWR 'B' Set, to run down the incline siding with the guard applying the brakes before hitting the buffer stops. The loco would then re-couple ready for the journey back to Bridport. November 2007.

Maiden Newton station is 154 miles and 8 chains (248km) from Paddington via Swindon.

Dorchester West

Date Built	Railway/Design	Platforms	Passengers 2023–2024	Listed
1857	GWR/IKB	2	89,732	Grade II

Dorchester West station is a snapshot of faded GWR nineteenth-century glory, a fine station now reduced in status but still fulfilling a function for Dorset's county town, despite the now single main line.

Above: **Figure 41.** Seemingly, some stops needed to be pulled out with this Brunellian station building in competition with the LSWR one in the town. Anyway, the GWR and Brunel won as the LSWR building is no longer with us. Some spear fencing is extant. August 2016.

Right: **Figure 42.** The canopy at Dorchester West is much later, possibly around 1890, and reminiscent of the one at Castle Cary now. August 2016.

Dorchester West station is 161 miles and 63 chains (260.37km) from Paddington via Swindon.

2

Cotswolds: Worcester and Hereford

Some of the line from Wolvercote Junction near Oxford to Worcester Shrub Hill was reinstated with double track in 2011, having been singled in the 1970s. Some of the survey includes the post-2011 situation. This journey begins at Culham in Oxfordshire.

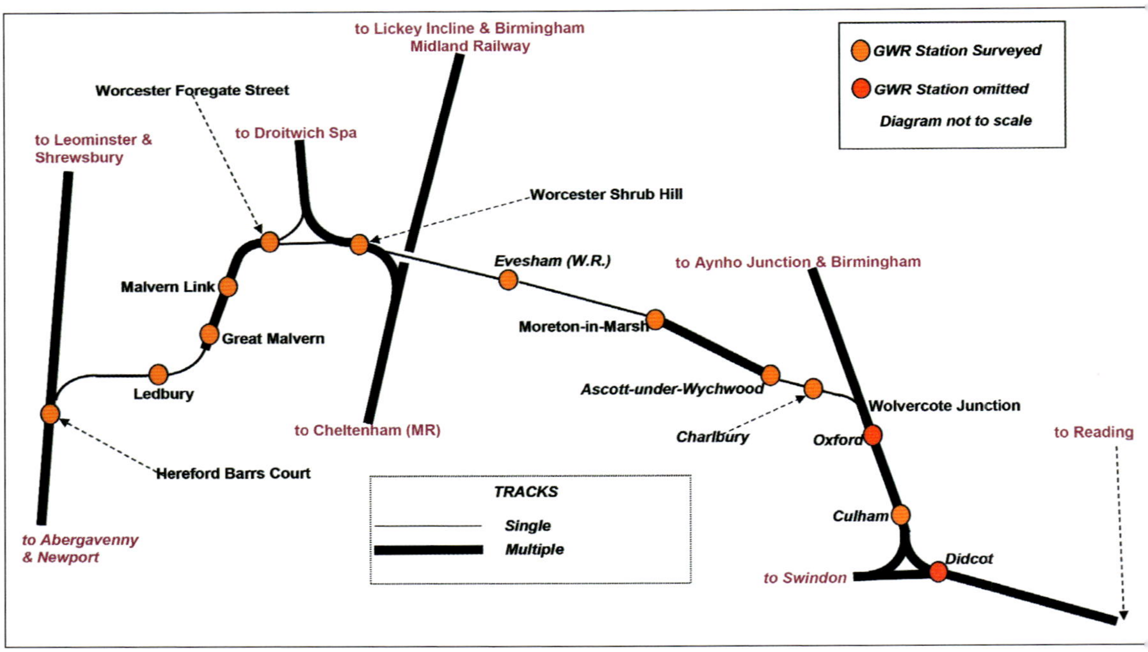

Figure 43. Cotswolds to Worcester and Hereford. The journey starts in Oxfordshire, meanders through Gloucestershire to Worcestershire, and finally Herefordshire.

Culham

Date Built	Railway/Design	Platforms	Passengers 2023–2024	Listed
1844	GWR/IKB	2	73,232	Grade II

What a Brunellian first Elizabethan-style gem in a largely modernised main line environment, and close to a former nuclear research installation. The station was a contemporary in the style of Pangbourne, Twyford and Yate and is the only survivor.

The station building was being inhabited by a graphic designer, who said he found much inspiration from such historic surroundings. The ornate embellishment of the awning is said to be at the behest of a local landowner. Much was done to placate and win over these powerful people, many of whom never wanted the railway until they got one. The stationmaster's house from a later period, around 1890, is also extant.

Figure 44. Culham was built to the same plan as three others but this is the sole survivor. The far chimney is for the ticket office and the near waiting room. The stationmaster's house is later and is of a typical pattern. Stationmasters were expected to be almost ever present and so a comfortable residence was provided. August 2016.

Figure 45. At Culham, the far door is the ticket office and some rooms are let to a graphic designer for an office and workshop. The left-hand end was an early toilet building, and is now a store. The post box dates from King George VI. August 2016.

Figure 46. The man with the graphic designer business was kind enough to allow a photograph of the former ticket office with cast iron fireplace. August 2016.

Culham station is 56 miles and 19 chains (90.5km) from Paddington.

Charlbury

Date Built	Railway/Design	Platforms	Passengers 2023–2024	Listed
1853	Oxford, Worcester and Wolverhampton IKB/John Fowler	1, 2 after 2011	0.275 million	Grade II

The original railway was known as the 'Old Worse and Worse' before its takeover by the GWR. There are still bridges in the locale with 'OW&W' labels painted on. An extremely rare Brunel-designed timber station building and now under the care of volunteers.

Figure 47. Sir Peter Parker, former chairman of the British Rail Board, used Charlbury station regularly and that was said to be a factor in the station's survival as well as the line's. However, the Italianate chalet-style building was listed along with platform furniture in a job lot. October 2003.

Figure 48. Charlbury in the pre-redoubling era sees the five listed platform seats still in business. The station and gardens were looked after by a local support group and the ornamental pond can just be seen behind the later railings. The over bridge in the distance was clearly built for double track and the whitewashed rectangle on the bridge denotes a sighting background for a semaphore signal, which had been controlled by the station's own signal box until 1971. The yellow mile post denotes 76 miles and 3 times 20 chains, or three quarters of a mile. October 2003.

Charlbury station is 76 miles and 60 chains (123.43km) from Paddington.

Ascott-under-Wychwood

Date Built	Railway/Design	Platforms	Passengers 2023–2024	Listed
1883 Signal box	GWR	1, 2 after 2011	1,392	No

Many of the buildings on the Oxford to Worcester line did not survive the singling and economies of the 1960s and 1970s. Here, the signal box survived as a block post passing trains from Oxford to Moreton-in-Marsh and supervising the crossing.

Figure 49. Ascott-under-Wychwood station was just a platform and bus shelter, but the signal box lives on to control the crossing and formerly to communicate with Moreton-in-Marsh for double-track working under the Absolute Block system. The signal box is reminiscent of the Mackenzie and Holland style of contractor signal box who supplied the GWR before they built their own at Reading signal works. October 2003.

Ascott-under-Wychwood station is 80 miles and 33 chains (129.41km) from Paddington.

Moreton-in-Marsh

Date Built	Railway/Design	Platforms	Passengers 2023–2024	Listed
1880s Rebuilt	OWW/GWR	2 in use	0.295 million	No

Moreton-in-Marsh is a pretty town on the edge of the Cotswolds, and the former junction station and its environs match the attractiveness of the borough. Modernisation has done its work but all the elements of a station, small goods shed, signal box and semaphore signals remain. Moreton-in-Marsh has seen an upsurge in tickets sold, contradicting the usual post Covid-19 scene. There are some station information signs in Japanese for the tourists on their way to Bibury and Bourton-on-the-Water. The village of Adlestrop, made famous by Edward Thomas' poem about the station, is nearby and in the listed bus shelter is the station nameboard and platform seat from Adelstrop station.

Figure 50. Moreton-in-Marsh station, and in the distance is the up line onwards to Oxford. The white building on the left was Moreton-in- Marsh creamery and was rail served. The platform where the GWR 'Siphon' milk vans were handled is clearly visible. Carrying on from the creamery and behind the left-hand platform was the loop platform for the Shipston-on-Stour passenger trains until 1929. March 2004.

Above: **Figure 51.** Fast forward ten years and the scene has changed somewhat. The HST has the 'off' for Oxford and Paddington but is still loading passengers. The small goods lockup on the left is now a Network Rail depot. The smaller semaphore signal on the left is a recent (2011) innovation since the track was doubled to Evesham. The signal enables a train to depart from the left-hand platform over the crossover to Oxford. The siding accommodating the yellow tamper machine has been lifted and the goods siding and cattle dock trackwork have gone (see Figure 54). The view is towards Evesham from the Oxford Road Bridge. September 2014.

Opposite above: **Figure 52.** Moreton-in-Marsh station building is reminiscent of the London suburban stations with yellow London bricks, decorative orange bricks and blue trimming bricks. Sash windows have survived but the chimneys and slate roof have not. April 2016.

Opposite below: **Figure 53.** GWR seats with cast and timber ends abound here, and the small detail that has survived is the blue painted iron fire bucket frame on this end of the building near the 'Gents'. September 2016.

Information
LONDON ATTRACTIONS 2FOR1 OFFERS
aXpressos
Buses to Chipping Campden, Stow-on-the-Wold & Bourton-on-the-Water

Above: **Figure 54.** This is the Oxford end at Moreton-in-Marsh, looking east. At this time there were still the vestiges of the cattle dock on the extreme right, and the short siding has the sleepers covered in brick with a cast iron grill to enable hosing down of the area after the cattle's departure. The tamper machine is sitting in the siding that had been the loop for the Shipston-on-Stour branch line. March 2004.

Opposite above: **Figure 55.** Networker Turbo Class 166, 166216 heads for Oxford past the down refuge siding, with its unusual single-railed trap point and subsidiary starting signal. March 2004.

Opposite below: **Figure 56.** The double track to Evesham curves away under this splendid bridge in Cotswold stone. The modern ground signal on the right is to signal a reversing move over a trailing crossover, whilst signal MM 5 is the down platform starter signal, suitably distanced from the platform to accommodate HST sets. April 2016.

166 216

MM
5

Figure 57. Part of the lever frame inside Moreton-in-Marsh signal box. The blue lever is a facing point lock and these were often left unlocked, as shown, so that a point could be changed over and then the lock replaced. The red levers are for signals, smaller cut down are for colour lights, black for points and white for unused. The small diagram is of the track layout when the Shipston branch was in operation prior to 1960. March 2004.

Moreton-in-Marsh station is 91 miles and 61 chains (147.68km) from Paddington.

Evesham

Date Built	Railway/Design	Platforms	Passengers 2023–2024	Listed
1880s Rebuilt	OWW/GWR	2	0.258 million	No

The beautiful Vale of Evesham is home to many fruit farms and growers, and Evesham may be said to be its jewel. At any rate, it attracted the Midland Railway to almost equal the GWR's facilities, but it is the latter that has survived.

Figure 58. Evesham station, and the view is towards Worcester when it was the end of the single-track section from Moreton-in-Marsh, and the start of the double track onwards. March 2004.

Figure 59. The single track from Moreton-in-Marsh splits into two for the platforms at Evesham from 1971–2011. The centre-balanced arm signal at the bottom of the picture is the up-platform starter, but has been moved over to this side of the tracks for train driver sighting reasons. March 2004.

Figure 60. The main station building at Evesham is quite impressive for a small town, but Evesham had a duplicate set alongside in the guise of the LMS (former Midland Railway) station. March 2004.

Figure 61. The up-platform station building at Evesham is slightly less grand, but is still looking after passengers. The dark rectangle beyond the over bridge is the signal box controlling some semaphores at this point. March 2004.

Figure 62. The footbridge at Evesham provides this vantage point of the east end of Evesham with some sidings remaining and goods buildings. March 2004.

Figure 63. After re-doubling between Evesham and Moreton-in-Marsh, Evesham lost its semaphore signals. The box dates from the 1950s and the W.R. on the box name was to distinguish it from the London Midland Region box which was nearby. The former LMS (Midland Railway) station ran alongside and was very similar to the GWR version. September 2014.

Evesham station is 106 miles and 55 chains (171.7km) from Paddington.

Worcester Shrub Hill

Date Built	Railway/Design	Platforms	Passengers 2023–2024	Listed
1865 Rebuilt	OWW/GWR Edward Wilson	3, 2 into 2 parts	0.527 million	Grade II (Parts)

Worcester is a lovely county city with a splendid cathedral but is, or was, also home to Lea & Perrins Sauce (the vinegar branch of old), Worcester Porcelain and a railway signal works. The railway scene is delightfully complicated by the lines running to it and how they approach the city. Semaphore signalling still mostly holds sway here, as well as other historical GWR features.

Above: **Figure 64.** The main building at Worcester Shrub Hill could pass for the Georgian period and is unique among the GWR's stations. The telephone box is a K6 and is listed. November 2008.

Opposite above: **Figure 65.** Platform 1 at Worcester Shrub Hill has the Hereford bay platform at the far end, now a car park. By the footbridge steps is a semaphore banjo signal, now unique on Network Rail; there had been another at Gloucester Central. Another signalling rarity is the black-faced ground signal with the yellow stripe. This means a train can pass straight without the signal needing to be changed over. If the crossover is to be taken, the signal must be selected 'OFF' or go to proceed. The 1960s K8 telephone kiosk on the platform is also listed. November 2016.

Opposite below: **Figure 66.** The footbridge affords this view towards Oxford with platform 1 on the right, at the end of which is Worcester Shrub Hill signal box. (See Figure 70 to see this end of the station in operation.) The red building on platform 2 on the left is the listed and recently restored waiting room. The walls that rise above the canopies on both sides supported the overall roof that was removed in 1930. The saw-toothed roof just past the signal box is part of the massive goods shed, now in other use for freight motor vehicles at the survey date. November 2016.

2a

Figure 67. Platform 3 on the right can just about accommodate a two-car DMU, so is not much used, although it had been a through-loop platform. The freight yard on the right is still used by trains that must reverse at Worcester, and for the parking of crippled wagons that have had to be removed from a train. Class 166 in platform 1 and class 47 on the middle siding. November 2008.

Figure 68. An iconic view of semaphore signals at Worcester Shrub Hill. The tracks round to the right are for Droitwich Spa and the West Midlands, and to the left, Hereford. The 'cash register' signal on the right is now unique on Network Rail and had signalled three destinations, the other being 'LOCO'. November 2016.

Figure 69. The Droitwich tracks were also the route to the steam engine sheds, coded 85A by British Railways, by Tunnel Junction signal box. The diesel servicing and refuelling depot is now in the crook of the junction. The line to Hereford on the left becomes single track within a short distance and the bracket signal on the far-left signals movements off the single line. The small semaphore signal on the right that is 'off' controls entry to the sidings for a freight train in an emergency. A ground frame enables a crew member to replace the signal to danger to protect the train. November 2008.

Figure 70. The vista from the Perry Wood Walk overbridge, adjacent to the former Metal Box factory, is of an Oxford-bound HST leaving platform 1 at Shrub Hill, and snaking over the crossover by the box to gain the up main line for Evesham. Both main platforms are bi-directionally signalled. The goods sidings are on the right. The crossovers in the foreground partly form what was Wylde's Lane Junction. The Metal Box factory was to the right nearer the camera. January 2016.

Worcester Shrub Hill station is 120 miles and 42 chains (194km) from Paddington via Didcot and Oxford.

Worcester Foregate Street

Date Built	Railway/Design	Platforms	Passengers 2023–2024	Listed
1860	GWR	2	1.748 million	No

Foregate Street is a major thoroughfare in the heart of the city, and sees approximately three times the passengers than its larger Shrub Hill cousin. It was built elevated above the city. Originally, it was all double track, but some of it is now single lines. The venerable Henwick Level Crossing signal box supervises working hereabouts after the platform signal box was closed.

Above: **Figure 71.** Foregate Street station is built on a viaduct in the centre of the city, and so has remained pretty much the same over the years. The bridge proudly bears the GWR coat of arms and the advertised Café Loco on the platform was a signal box. November 2016.

Opposite above: **Figure 72.** The view from platform 2 at Foregate Street emphasises the curving and elevated nature of the station. The bridge from the previous figure can be seen at the end of the far platform. November 2016.

Opposite below: **Figure 73.** Café Loco at Worcester Foregate was formerly a signal box and was doing brisk business at the time of the visit. Confirmation of the single line running arrangements is in the form of two notices. One on the end each platform, warning that trains may come and go, on either line in either direction. Platform 1 sees the departure of this class 172, 172220 London Midland service from Shrub Hill. November 2016.

CAUTION
TWO-WAY
working on
BOTH LINES
Café Loco
MIND THE STEP
MIND

Figure 74. The class 172 departs for Malvern over the viaduct and the signalling, controlled from Henwick LC signal box, is indicative of the fact that there are two single lines here. The right-hand line is for trains coming from and going to Droitwich Spa and missing out Shrub Hill. November 2016.

Figure 75. The opposite direction view to the previous figure continues the two single lines theme, with the left-hand track going to Droitwich and the right hand to Shrub Hill. The yellow distant signal arm is fixed at caution. November 2016.

Worcester Foregate Street station is 121 miles and 12 chains (194.97km) from Paddington via Didcot and Oxford.

Malvern Link

Date Built	Railway/Design	Platforms	Passengers 2023–2024	Listed
1859	GWR	2	0.317 million	No

Malvern Link was not as exalted as its neighbour, Great Malvern, and might be said to be more workaday. The stations are just over a mile apart and both do good business, both seeing passenger increases after the pandemic. Much of Malvern Link was demolished, and the current station is a modern reconstruction in the style and character of the GWR.

Figure 76. Malvern Link was recently reconstructed in the GWR style by the local authority and the Railway Heritage Trust. With a genuine footbridge and platform furniture, the station looks the part and has won an award from the local civic society. There is some evidence of whitewashed rectangles on the road bridge to improve semaphore signal sighting. January 2016.

Figure 77. Possibly the only original part of Malvern Link station is the stationmaster's residence on the left, but the replica running in board on the right keeps it company. The direction of travel is towards Great Malvern. January 2016.

Malvern Link station is 127 miles and 75 chains (205.9km) from Paddington.

Great Malvern

Date Built	Railway/Design	Platforms	Passengers 2023–2024	Listed
1859	GWR E.W. Elmslie	2	0.401 million	Grade II

Great Malvern is famous as a spa, which in Victorian times was prized as a curative for the ills of the Industrial Revolution, as well as a fount of eminently drinkable mineral water. The mineral water survives at a free spring head, where locals take their plastic bottles to fill up. The station would be endowed by the wealthy Lady Emily Foley, a relative of the Dukes of Montrose, and she insisted on her own private waiting room at the station, now a café. It was not uncommon to have 1st, 2nd and 3rd class waiting rooms at the larger stations. Malvern is also associated with the composer Sir Edward Elgar, and a Castle Class 4-6-0 locomotive, 7005, was named as such in 1957.

Above: **Figure 78.** Great Malvern is a total one-off in GWR station architecture. A magnificent exuberance of French gothic Victorian wealth, decoration and detail. This was not all. There was an elegant porte *cochère* or hansom cab type car port until about 30 years ago. January 2016.

Opposite above: **Figure 79.** Great Malvern platform 1, on the right, has a superb canopy supported by bespoke cast iron columns. The cast iron work around the subway is almost worthy of the Art Nouveau style of the Metro in Paris. The café on platform 1 was the private waiting room of a wealthy Victorian woman. January 2016.

Opposite below: **Figure 80.** More of the ironwork at Great Malvern is pictured together with more platform furniture. Note the GWR barrow down the platform and the clock says B.R. (W) for British Railways Western Region. The alternate-coloured stonework around the doorways is particularly fine. Platform 2 houses a second-hand bookshop. January 2016.

Figure 81. A vignette at Great Malvern, centred on the Pooley weighbridge for the weighing of parcels and platform trolley upon which to transport the loaded parcels. Platform seats are in the 1894 and 1934 styles, with all-wooden versions on platform 2. January 2016.

Figure 82. On platform 2 is this covered walkway, known as the 'Worm', which extends to a building on the far left, out of shot. The building was originally the Imperial Hotel and latterly a school. These passengers had their own private, sheltered route to access the station. January 2016.

Great Malvern station is 129 miles and 6 chains (207.73km) from Paddington. After Great Malvern and then Malvern Wells signal box, the line resumes on single track through Colwall and on to Ledbury in Herefordshire.

Ledbury

Date Built	Railway/Design	Platforms	Passengers 2023–2024	Listed
1885 Signal box	West Midland Railway / GWR	2	0.185 million	No

Ledbury was a junction with a branch line to Gloucester, subsequently closed in 1959. In steam days, a small locomotive depot and turntable existed to house banking engines used to assist mainly freight trains through Ledbury Tunnel. The signal box works the unique 'Lock and Block' telegraphic system through Ledbury Tunnel to Malvern Wells signal box. The single line other direction to Hereford is BR Western Region Tokenless Block working.

Figure 83. Ledbury signal box supervises working through the 1,316-yard (1,203m) Ledbury Tunnel, using a now-unique ancient technology. The system has provided single-line working avoiding collisions for many years. The London Midland class 170 on the right, 170632 has arrived from Great Malvern, and this has enabled the signaller to pull off the two semaphore signals to enable the Worcester-bound service to depart on the left. There are two starting signals to accommodate the greater length of HST sets, as well as DMUs. January 2016.

Ledbury station is 136 miles and 9 chains (219.05km) from Paddington.

Hereford Barrs Court

Date Built	Railway/Design	Platforms	Passengers 2023–2024	Listed
1856	Hereford, Ross and Gloucester John Penson	4	1.16 million	No

Hereford is another fine county city with a well-known cathedral housing the medieval *Mappa Mundi*. The Midland Railway also found its way to the city with a station and goods yards at Barton, and the name survives as a former junction label but little else. Hereford was the ultimate destination of the Cathedrals Express in steam days, that called at Oxford and Worcester on the way, and was one of the last steam-hauled named trains, usually by a Castle but sometimes by a Modified Hall class loco, which were considered almost as good.

Figure 84. Another neo-gothic Victorian treat, in the guise of Hereford Barrs Court. The name was to distinguish between the LMS Midland Railway edifice at Barton. A fitting terminus for the Cathedrals Express. The goods shed survives in the distance, in other use. October 2016.

Figure 85. The view is looking south towards Newport and South Wales. The bay platform 4 on the right services Birmingham terminating trains, whilst a London Midland service to Worcester waits in platform 1 on the left. October 2016.

Figure 86. Paddington bound HST arrives at platform 3 at Hereford. The signal box controls rod worked points and semaphore ground signals. October 2016.

Above: **Figure 87.** Class 60 and EWS steel trains for Shotton in North Wales are usually routed to the centre roads, but perhaps the driver can admire the island platform ironwork and footbridge at Hereford. April 2005.

Opposite above: **Figure 88.** Just the other side of the Aylestone Hill bridge at Hereford, looking south, are the Edgar Street sidings. More ground signals and a rod worked point on the down line are on the right, with facing point lock. The 'Cider Branch' that lead to Bulmer's Cider works and the early preservation of GWR King George V is still in being. April 2005.

Opposite below: **Figure 89.** The goods shed at Hereford has survived as a bowling alley. The track right in front of the goods shed is the platform 4 bay. Notice that the wagon entrance way is of broad-gauge dimensions. October 2016.

Mileages change here from Paddington to Shrewsbury. Hereford Barrs Court station is 51 miles and 3 chains (82.14km) from English Bridge Junction, Shrewsbury.

3

Wolverhampton to Chester

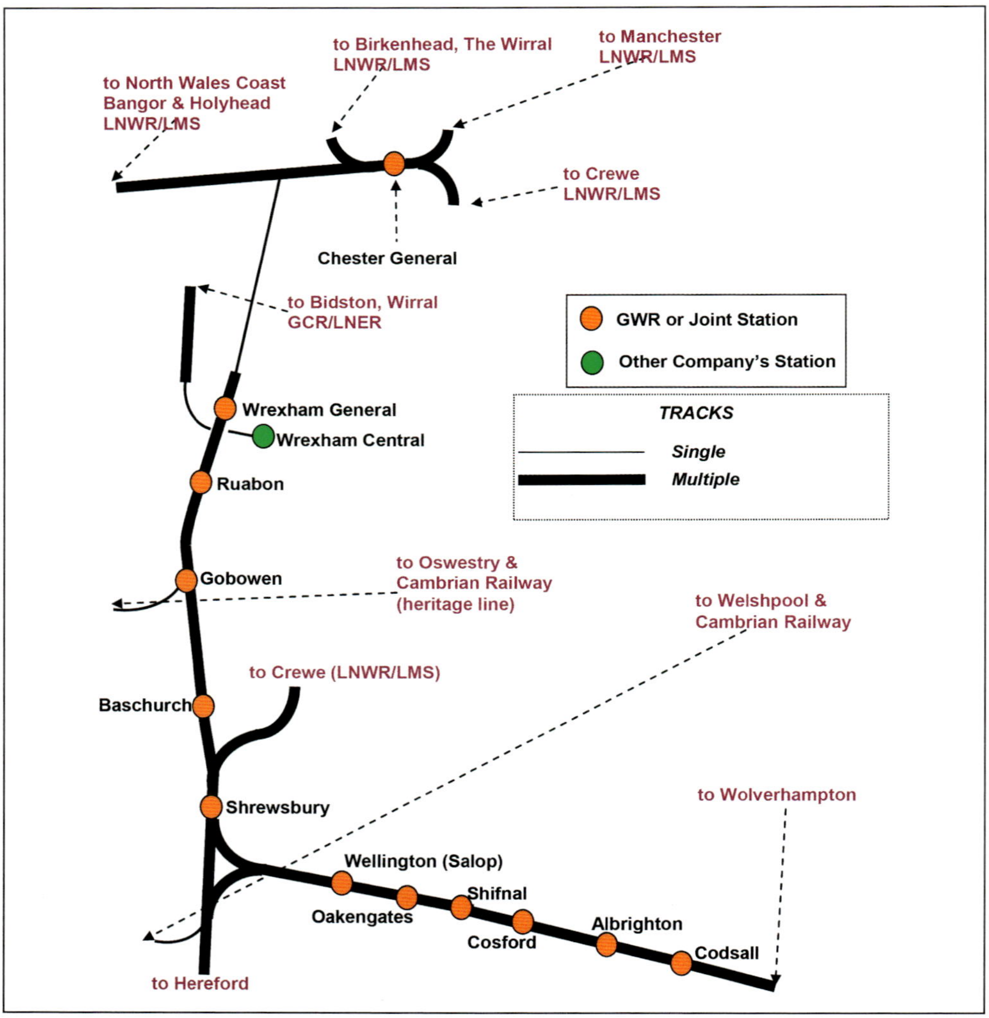

Figure 90. Wolverhampton to Chester General. The journey moves from the 'Black Country' through leafy Shropshire to Roman Deva or Chester.

There are some joint stations here, as the northern area of the Welsh Marches tended to adopt the joint approach rather than have separate stations for the companies. Figure 90 attempts to illustrate the mixture of railway companies there were. The line crosses the Welsh border soon after Gobowen but regains England after Wrexham.

Codsall

Date Built	Railway/Design	Platforms	Passengers 2023–2024	Listed
1850	Shrewsbury and Birmingham Railway	2	0.122 million	Grade II and footbridge

Codsall station is close enough to Wolverhampton to be a commuter base. The main station building is a CAMRA recognised pub known as The Station. The signal box depicted in one of the views has been taken out of service and removed to the Dean Forest Railway preserved line.

Figure 91. Codsall station building was a pub and restaurant at the survey date and contains much railway memorabilia. The GWR splasher-type nameplate announces 'HOLDEN'S BREWERY'. The pub remains in 2025 and has won many CAMRA awards. April 2005.

Above: **Figure 92.** The listed footbridge is dated 1883 and was damaged by contractors in an accident two months after the visit. The footbridge has subsequently been repaired with replica castings done locally, but is now a slightly larger aperture to accommodate the modern loading gauge. April 2005.

Opposite above: **Figure 93.** The view towards Wolverhampton reveals a GWR timber signal box and LMR upper quadrant signals. Further up the line, there are GWR pattern semaphore signals. Codsall's were removed in 2006/7. Note the typical GWR running in board in the pub car park. April 2005.

Opposite below: **Figure 94.** The platform waiting shelter at Codsall may have lost its roof in a fire, so is a bit of a hybrid. April 2005.

Codsall station is 146 miles and 41 chains (235.79km) from Paddington via Oxford and Birmingham Snow Hill station.

Albrighton

Date Built	Railway/Design	Platforms	Passengers 2023–2024	Listed
1849	Shrewsbury and Birmingham Railway	2	91,340	Grade II and footbridge

Albrighton is an upmarket village, also on the Wolverhampton commuter route but now in Shropshire. Confusingly, there is another Albrighton in the county near Shrewsbury. It is also the local village for RAF Cosford and, historically, there was service accommodation here in the form of married quarters.

Left: **Figure 95.** A smaller but similar Italianate pattern station building at Albrighton. April 2005.

Below: **Figure 96.** Following the success of The Station pub at Codsall, Albrighton is following suit with an Ale House but, unlike Codsall, the Ale House did not survive. To the left is the Wolverhampton direction. July 2016.

Figure 97. The up platform waiting room and facilities at Albrighton are quite comprehensive, if no longer in use. April 2005.

Figure 98. The footbridge at Albrighton is similar to Codsall, even to the date of 1883, but without the trauma of a crane smashing into it, as at Codsall. The direction of travel away from the camera is towards Shrewsbury. July 2016.

Albrighton station is 149 miles and 38 chains (240.56km) from Paddington via Oxford and Birmingham Snow Hill station.

Cosford

Date Built	Railway/Design	Platforms	Passengers 2023–2024	Listed
1938 March	GWR	2	71,394	No

The station was built and named 'Cosford Aerodrome Halt' to service RAF Cosford, then being built, and although the waiting shelters and original platforms were economic timber, the station building was brick built, probably later. There were goods loops and a signal box, as well as a connection to the air base for supplies, principally coal for the camp's central-heating system. The station was modified in 1942 with 600ft-long platforms. The unit was principally an engineering training base and hospital, and also now houses an aircraft museum.

Figure 99. Cosford was built as a World War II expedient on an embankment, and the former ticket office is down below at road level on the left. The brick based/timber top signal box was later dismantled and donated mostly to the Gloucestershire and Warwickshire Steam Railway heritage outfit. April 2005.

Figure 100. Cosford ticket office is viewed from road level, now in other use. Despite the nation facing impending doom in World War II, there is a fair bit of decoration and pride. April 2005.

Figure 101. Cosford station building supporting piles are seen here, as we can just see a class 66 and empty coal train head south from Ironbridge power station. The semaphore signal is a BR WR post supporting a London Midland Region upper quadrant arm. April 2005.

Figure 102. The waiting shelters and timber-built platforms at Cosford haven't survived, and the facilities here were as spartan as the GWR descended to—not even a fire to warm the waiting passengers. Such were the exigencies of war time. April 2005.

Cosford station is 151 miles and 7 chains (243.15km) from Paddington via Oxford and Birmingham Snow Hill station.

Shifnal

Date Built	Railway/Design	Platforms	Passengers 2023–2024	Listed
1890 circa	GWR	2	0.173 million	No

Shifnal had been a coaching station in the earlier nineteenth century, with the journey from London taking 27 hours, until the use of 150 horses en route slashed this to 16½ hours. Shifnal is also a commuter base for Telford, as well as Wolverhampton.

Figure 103. Shifnal station building looks to be of the standard 1890s pattern, which would have been current when the station was opened, and much changed. It looks like the Gents toilet was at this end. July 2016.

Shifnal station is 154 miles and 24 chains (248.32km) from Paddington via Oxford and Birmingham Snow Hill station.

Oakengates

Date Built	Railway/Design	Platforms	Passengers 2023–2024	Listed
1849	Shrewsbury and Birmingham Railway	2	71,524	No

Oakengates has a rich and varied history, from the early production of pig iron using coke rather than charcoal to innovations in the canal industry. Oakengates Market Street station was an early closure casualty in 1952, as part of the Coalport branch line.

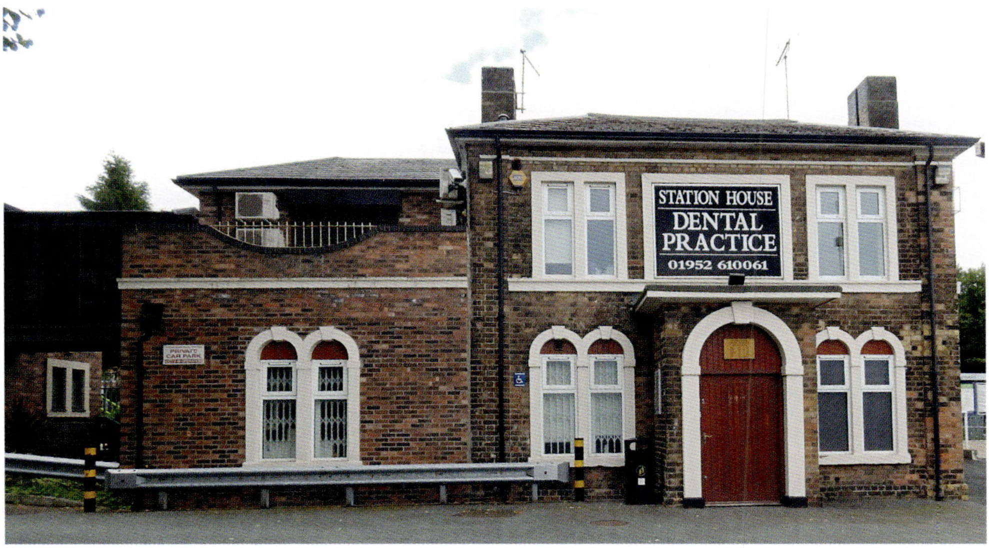

Above: **Figure 104.** Although in other use now, Oakengates station building retains much of its original character. July 2016.

Right: **Figure 105.** The cut-down footbridge is the only other GWR fragment here at Oakengates. July 2016.

Oakengates station is 158 miles and 31 chains (240.56km) from Paddington via Oxford and Birmingham Snow Hill station.

Wellington (Shropshire)

Date Built	Railway/Design	Platforms	Passengers 2023–2024	Listed
1849	GWR	3 (was 6)	0.606 million	No

Wellington is another venerable market town, but has now been recognised as part of Telford new town. The railway picture was complicated by a branch line from Stafford, owned by the London and North Western Railway (later LMSR) and hence making the station a joint one. There were two other branch lines running in, one from Market Drayton, Nantwich and Crewe, and another from that crucible of the Industrial Revolution, Coalbrookdale, as well as Coalport. Part of the latter has become the Horsehay Steam Railway. This branch went onto a junction at Buildwas, for what is now the iconic Severn Valley Railway and Much Wenlock. All three branch lines closed in the 1960s.

Above: **Figure 106.** The bay for Craven Arms and Much Wenlock was on the extreme left and the bays were part of the 1881 rebuilding. The platform on the right had been an island, and Wellington loco depot (closed 1964) was further up the car park. The Cambrian Coast Express would thunder through the station on the centre tracks. The view is towards Shrewsbury. December 2016.

Opposite above: **Figure 107.** The main station building at Wellington is now unique on the former GWR and hemmed in by the cutting in which the station sits. The hotel on the right, now named Carriages, was an early buffet/restaurant for travellers. December 2016.

Opposite below: **Figure 108.** The main station buildings at Wellington have a tower at each end that exudes solidity and worth of a junction and joint station. December 2016.

Wellington
Information
The Station
BREAKFAST

Figure 109. One of the towers is used as the entrance way for the footbridge. The alternate colouring is reminiscent of Great Malvern but here uses stone and brick. Platform seats are early GWR monogram and BR (W), and both types look to be original castings. December 2016.

Figure 110. The island platform building appears to be later (at around 1890) but seems to fit in. The bay platform 3 (originally LMS for Stafford) is now disused after trains to Walsall were discontinued in 2008. December 2016.

Wellington station is 161 miles and 27 chains (259.65km) from Paddington via Oxford and Birmingham Snow Hill station.

Shrewsbury

Date Built	Railway/Design	Platforms	Passengers 2023–2024	Listed
1848	Shrewsbury and Chester Railway	5 (3–7 incl.)	2.013 million	Grade II

Shrewsbury is a delightful medieval town and administrative centre for the county of Shropshire. It is also a meeting point of several railways and a considerable junction. The station was jointly owned with the London and North Western Railway. Part of this was the signalling, where LNWR and GWR signal boxes together with mostly GWR signals controlled the complex track layout. Coleham locomotive depot was a large joint facility and as such, in BR days, hosted a mixture of former GWR and LMS types, as well as BR Standard classes.

The station and area passed from the Western Region to the London Midland Region in September 1963, further complicating the scene and enhancing the variety to be found. Platforms 1 and 2 had been bay platforms to service the Severn Valley and Cambrian local lines. Crewe works used to send ex-works LMS express passenger locomotives to Shrewsbury as a running in turn.

Figure 111. The magnificent Tudor-style station building at Shrewsbury was said to cost £100,000 when new in 1848, but has been a lasting legacy to railway grandeur of a complicated junction and joint station. The brick-built walkway on the right leads to a footbridge that crosses all platforms, and ends up in Howard Street by the former prison and named after the prison reformer. December 2016.

Above: **Figure 112.** At the top of the footpath, leading to the footbridge as described in the previous figure, is this view. The double tracks are headed north for Chester with a line to Coton Hill goods on the left. The building above the white-hatted track worker is the former GWR Castle Foregate goods depot, in other use. December 2016.

Opposite above: **Figure 113.** The view from Howard Street and the footbridge referred to in the previous figure is centre stage, and below is the island platform and building that contains two bay platforms on the left. Platform 7 is nearest the camera, followed by the goods-avoiding loop and a siding to a loading dock nearest of all. The walls on both sides supported the overall roof, which was removed in the 1960s. Shrewsbury Castle overlooks the scene and had its own Castle Class loco named after it, No 5009. December 2016.

Opposite below: **Figure 114.** The view is from the footbridge looking south. The listed Severn Bridge Junction signal box, now the largest mechanical box in the world at 180 levers, sits in the middle of a triangle, where the tracks to the right go to Sutton Bridge Junction, where the line splits again towards the Cambrian and Hereford. To the left, the tracks go to Wellington. Although the box is of LNWR origin, much of the equipment within is of GWR origin. On the far right, the overall roof support wall was the location of platforms 1 and 2, which were used by Severn Valley trains. Shrewsbury Abbey is the ideal train-spotting venue. December 2016.

Above: **Figure 115.** Towards the north end, the tracks are Chester bound and also curve round to the right for the Crewe line. The listed Crewe Junction signal box is just in view, and appears to be shorter than Severn Bridge, but is in fact taller as it descends to street level. Further up the Crewe line is the LMS Crewe Bank signal box. December 2016.

Opposite above: **Figure 116.** The Crewe line curves round to the right and Chester beckons to the left. All signals except one are GWR pattern lower quadrant. January 2015.

Opposite below: **Figure 117.** At the south end of the station, the carriage sidings are in the foreground and the tracks from the left come in from Wellington. The two tracks that loop away to the upper left are freight-avoiding lines that join up with the Hereford/Cambrian lines before Sutton Bridge Junction. Down signals are upper quadrant, up are lower quadrant, and see the GWR manual point lever with guard rail to the right in the carriage sidings. In earlier years there had been gantries of signals instead of brackets. January 2004.

Shrewsbury station is 171 miles and 46 chains (276.12km) from Paddington via Oxford and Birmingham Snow Hill station.

Baschurch

Date Built	Railway/Design	Platforms	Passengers	Listed
1848	Shrewsbury and Chester Railway	Nil in use	Closed in 1960	Grade II

Baschurch station appears abandoned now, but had been busy with two signal boxes, two platforms and a goods yard. In 1961, an unfitted freight train, GWR 28XX hauled, was being shunted into a refuge siding when it was hit by a down express passenger train, hauled by a 4-6-0 Hall Class locomotive, headed for Wellington. The resulting collision caused the death of three railway servants and around twenty injuries. There is a popular movement to have the station reopened.

Above: **Figure 118.** Baschurch is about 8 miles north of Shrewsbury on the Chester line. The station building had the Tudor-type chimneys removed before it was listed. This style of architecture was typical of the Shrewsbury and Chester Railway. April 2005.

Opposite above: **Figure 119.** At Baschurch there's a job lot of listings with the signal box (1880), station building and ivy-covered water-pumping tower. The latter was a facility for the village and farmers, and fresh water was a valuable resource provided by many railway companies. December 2016.

Opposite below: **Figure 120.** The ornate chimneys as well as the finials have survived on the crossing keeper's cottage at Baschurch, and so has the BR (WR) era signal post which is also listed. July 2016.

Baschurch station crossing is 179 miles and 14 chains (288.35km) from Paddington via Oxford.

Gobowen

Date Built	Railway/Design	Platforms	Passengers 2023–2024	Listed
1849	Shrewsbury and Chester Railway T.W. Penson	2 in use, 3 present	0.218 million	Grade II

Gobowen is the junction for the GWR branch line to Oswestry, the headquarters of the Cambrian Railway. There were a group of sidings to handle, mostly junction goods traffic, for and off the Cambrian, under the control of Gobowen South signal box, now gone. Gobowen North signal box survives, as it controls the level crossing as well as the semaphore signals and colour lights that remain. The Cambrian Heritage Railway vows to restore services on the remaining track to Oswestry and beyond, but the A5 safe-road crossing presents an obstacle.

Above: **Figure 121.** The Italianate design of Gobowen station emphasised its status as a junction for the line to Oswestry and connection to the Cambrian Railway. November 2016.

Opposite above: **Figure 122.** The building on the up platform is somewhat more modest, but now houses a travel/ticket agency, run by a local girls' school, and a thriving café. The station running in board is also listed. November 2016.

Opposite below: **Figure 123.** The characteristic round-topped canopies for narrower platforms are both in place, and the Oswestry shuttle with auto trailer and fitted 48/14XX locomotive departed from the left-hand bay platform. Although other motive power was used in later years, and if the regular set was in the nearby works. Alongside the bay platform track was a coal yard that was operating well into the 2000s. November 2016.

Gobowen

Figure 124. An Arriva Trains class 158, 158822 is drifting to a halt over the crossing past Gobowen North signal box with a train from Chester. There are lower-quadrant GWR pattern signals on the up side, despite this station being part of the London Midland Region since September 1963. The preceding signal has already been replaced to danger in a smart piece of working. November 2014.

Figure 125. The motorised upper quadrant starter signal on the down platform at Gobowen gives the 'off' to a Chester-bound Arriva Coradia class 175 DMU, 175101.

The motorised signal is said to simplify arrangements with the connection to the box the other side of the crossing. Note the replica GWR gas lamp on the platform. November 2016.

Gobowen station is 189 miles and 50 chains (305.17km) from Paddington via Oxford.

Ruabon

Date Built	Railway/Design	Platforms	Passengers 2023–2024	Listed
1860	GWR Henry Robertson	2 (reduced)	97,222	No

Ruabon was the junction for the Ruabon to Dolgelley (Dolgellau) line. This line meandered delightfully for 54 miles across rural North/Mid Wales and included Llangollen as a major station, to which the line was double track and thereafter single. Ruabon had extensive fans of sidings, as there were collieries and brickworks hereabouts, and included a locomotive turntable. Red Ruabon brick was a byword for style and quality in the nineteenth century. Some of the site is overgrown but vestiges of a former glory remain. Much of the track bed was built on after closure, thus denying the likelihood of trains running from Ruabon to Llangollen again.

Figure 126. Ruabon looking south with a Chester-bound class 158 DMU, 158838 ready to depart from the former island platform. Note how the platform length has been cut back on both sides. The footbridge continues to the right, as if to span the now-removed twin tracks. December 2016.

Figure 127. The station building at Ruabon is later than the original creation by Penson, as the station expanded to accommodate the branch line to Dolgelley (Dolgellau). Part of this branch line is now the heritage Llangollen Railway and narrow-gauge Bala Lake Railway. December 2016.

Ruabon station is 197 miles and 4 chains (317.12km) from Paddington via Oxford.

Wrexham General

Date Built	Railway/Design	Platforms	Passengers 2023–2024	Listed
1875 Rebuilt	GWR	4	0.630 million	Grade II CADW

Wrexham attracted other railway companies, notably the Cambrian and the Great Central (latterly LNER) in their quest for a share of the minerals, mostly coal, in the area. The GWR held sway with a large locomotive depot, Croes Newydd, and several goods yards. The Great Central had Central and Exchange stations, as well as Rhosddu engine sheds and the Cambrian-shared Central. Wrexham General has a station building in the French style and is reminiscent of the long-gone Ross-on-Wye or the 1984-created Kidderminster on the Severn Valley Railway.

Above: **Figure 128.** Wrexham General station building is in the French Pavilion style and the main building is in stone. The brick-built Edwardian additions are also on view. The floodlights are for Wrexham FC's ground nearby. December 2016.

Opposite above: **Figure 129.** The view is south under the fine canopies at Wrexham General, and the restoration has been commemorated by blue plaques on the left. Beyond the over bridge and on the left are two additional bay platforms. Part of this bay area was a storage facility for the erstwhile Wrexham and Shropshire Railway trains. December 2016.

Opposite below: **Figure 130.** The view north from the road over bridge in the last figure and the modern extension to the footbridge is to platform 4, which had been a separate GCR/LNER station, Wrexham Exchange. North of the station, the line becomes single track but is in the process of reinstatement to double track, as it had been in GWR days. The steel train mentioned at Hereford Barrs Court would take the left-hand track to the ex-LNER route north. December 2016.

Figure 131. Beyond the over bridge and looking north again, the two tracks for the incognito bay platforms are on the left. In the distance is Croes Newydd North Fork signal box and a Shrewsbury and Chester Railway crossing keeper's cottage, now restored as a private dwelling. December 2016.

Figure 132. The darker brick-built goods shed with later red-brick-built office extension survives at Wrexham General, in use as a builder's merchant. The opposite end wall of the stone shed still has the painted remnants of the 'GREAT WEST.. GOODS..' advertising slogan, although not as complete as the example at Stroud. November 2004.

Wrexham General station is 201 miles and 66 chains (324.81km) from Paddington via Oxford.

Chester General

Date Built	Railway/Design	Platforms	Passengers 2023–2024	Listed
1847–8	Chester and Holyhead Francis Thompson	7 3 and 4 subdivided	4,727 million	Grade II

Chester General was an early joint station with the London and North Western Railway, with the GWR very much the junior partner. Lines run in from Manchester, Crewe, Holyhead and the Wirral to Birkenhead. The latter connection was a joint line with the GWR, to enable the company to reach Liverpool transatlantic liners via the Mersey Ferries. The LNER, in the form of the Great Central, kept a presence at the other station, Northgate, together with the Cheshire Lines Committee lines. There were three steam engine sheds at Chester, the LNWR and the GWR, of which only the latter survives as a much-modified DMU depot, and the earlier closed Northgate. The former GWR goods shed also survives in other use.

Figure 133. The magnificent Italianate frontage of Chester General station conceals a more modest interior, but Chester remains a rail hub in the northwest of England.

Thomas Brassey, a noted railway entrepreneur, is associated with the railways in the city. December 2016.

Figure 134. Beyond the yellow-fronted class 150 DMU on the right, the GWR passenger trains were serviced at platforms known as the 'Mold bay'. This meant that every train between Birkenhead and Paddington had to reverse here, and engines were changed, often from a Castle to a large Prairie tank engine and vice versa. The third rail in the foreground is for the extension of the electrified Merseyrail system. The view is east towards the Manchester and Crewe LMS lines. December 2016.

Chester General station is 179 miles and 11 chains (288.27km) from Euston station on the LNWR/LMS.

Droitwich Spa to Stourbridge Junction

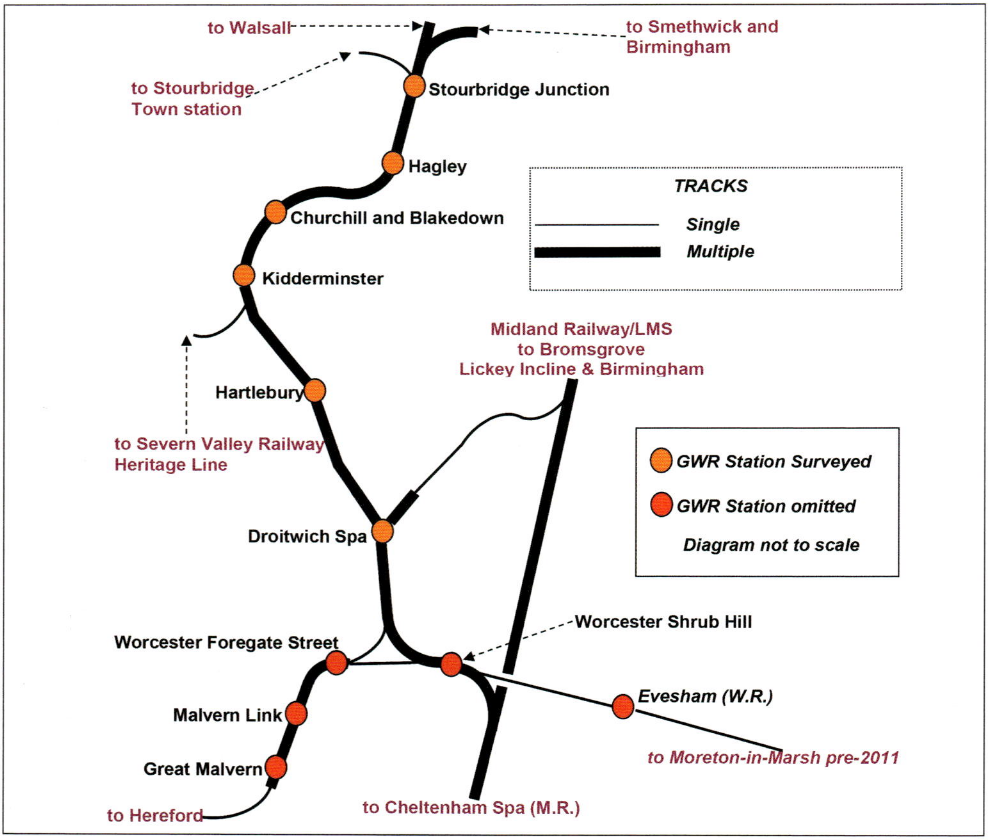

Figure 135. Droitwich Spa to Stourbridge Junction.

The line here starts off in the same semaphore-signalled time warp as Worcester, but has been progressively modernised as the tracks near Birmingham. Recent years have seen even greater modernisation, with upgrades to signalling consigning some of the GWR boxes to history, although the buildings survive in some cases. The journey starts in Worcestershire at Droitwich Spa and heads north (see Figure 135).

Droitwich Spa

Date Built	Railway/Design	Platforms	Passengers 2023–2024	Listed
1899 GWR Rebuilt	Oxford, Worcester and Wolverhampton	2	0.463 million	No

The town is similarly in the delightful style of Malvern, although with Roman origins—any town ending with the phrase 'wich' was a source of salt (Northwich, Nantwich and so on). Much of the station has not survived, but the fine junction signal box and signals are unmistakable GWR heritage evidence.

Figure 136. Not much of the GWR's 1899 station rebuild of the 'Old Worse and Worse' edifice has survived, but the junction north is still controlled by GWR pattern equipment, including the centre balanced signals on the platform. Class 150 DMU heads for Stourbridge Junction in the distance. January 2004.

Above: **Figure 137.** This is a closer view of the junction with three section signals 'off' for a train from Stourbridge. The smaller posted signals are for goods loops. January 2004.

Opposite above: **Figure 138.** What a difference a decade makes. The tall, posted signal nearest the camera has been replaced by a dumpier version on the more usual side of the tracks, and the down goods loop on the left is disappearing. July 2014.

Opposite below: **Figure 139.** This picture is a look back in time and in the direction of Worcester. The waiting shelter was part of the 1899 rebuild. January 2004.

Droitwich Spa station is 126 miles and 10 chains (202.98km) from Paddington via Didcot Oxford and Worcester.

Hartlebury

Date Built	Railway/Design	Platforms	Passengers 2023–2024	Listed
1870s GWR Rebuilt	Oxford, Worcester and Wolverhampton	2	50,794	No

Hartlebury Castle is a local landmark with ecclesiastical connections and a Castle Class locomotive, 7034, named after it. Nearby, was a junction with what is now the Severn Valley Railway, and the line also continues to reach Kidderminster, thereby forming a large triangle that involved Stourport.

Left: **Figure 140.** Hartlebury station, with the view towards Kidderminster, reveals another station building, which is now a pub/restaurant, and what appears to be a goods lockup, although somewhat modified. August 2016.

Below: **Figure 141.** Hartlebury signal box had been one of the oldest GWR signal boxes until its demise in 2012. Just by the crossover was the southern connection to the Severn Valley Railway in BR days. January 2006.

Hartlebury station is 131 miles and 68 chains (212.19km) from Paddington via Didcot, Oxford and Worcester.

Kidderminster

Date Built	Railway/Design	Platforms	Passengers 2023–2024	Listed
1852 Original	Oxford, Worcester and Wolverhampton	2	1.128 million	No

The delightful half-timbered station was lost in the 1960s. The massive goods shed, reputedly to handle large volumes of Kidderminster-manufactured carpet, survives as the Severn Valley's carriage works and shed. There had been a small locomotive depot in steam days that had an even smaller sub-shed at Hartlebury. The original ramshackle setup was updated with money from the 1929 Loan Guarantees and Grants Act.

Figure 142. The original OWW station of 1852 resembled a half-timbered pub, which succumbed to dry rot and was demolished in 1968. The waiting shelter on platform 2 was all that remained, looking towards Stourbridge. May 2006.

Figure 143. The GWR signal box at Kidderminster fared little better than the station building, as it had been demolished by an errant goods train. Its Festival of Britain style BR replacement is seen here with a sand drag for protection from the siding exit on the upside. The ground signal on the bottom right of the picture belongs to the Severn Valley Railway. August 2006.

Kidderminster station is 135 miles and 46 chains (218.19km) from Paddington via Didcot, Oxford and Worcester.

Churchill and Blakedown

Date Built	Railway/Design	Platforms	Passengers 2023–2024	Listed
1888 Signal box	Oxford, Worcester and Wolverhampton	2	97,028	No

Churchill and Blakedown signal box is all that has survived here. The local people loved their signal box so much that they paid to have it moved off railway property when the signal box closed and have it refurbished.

Figure 144. Villagers at Blakedown were horrified to learn that 'their' signal box was to be closed and demolished. Negotiations took place and the signal box was dismantled and reassembled slightly away from the running lines and the road crossing. August 2016.

Blakedown station is 138 miles and 54 chains (223.18km) from Paddington via Didcot, Oxford and Worcester.

Hagley

Date Built	Railway/Design	Platforms	Passengers 2023–2024	Listed
1884 GWR Rebuilt	Oxford, Worcester and Wolverhampton	2	0.440 million	Grade II footbridge

In the twenty-first century, there are few wayside passenger stations that have survived almost intact as Hagley. Hagley Hall is nearby and perhaps there was some influence from that direction. The Hall Class locomotive of the name and numbered 4930 is preserved at the nearby Severn Valley Railway. In 2011, the station was repainted in the GWR structure colours of light and dark stone and Hornby Railways used the footbridge as a template for their 00-scale model.

Above: **Figure 145.** The GWR logo and build date of 1884 are picked out in dark stone against a light stone background on the footbridge at Hagley. August 2016.

Right: **Figure 146.** The station building at Hagley survives with some sash windows and ornate cast iron bracketry. August 2016.

Figure 147. The top of the footbridges with corrugated iron roofs was painted in black gas tar, but the inside at Hagley is lighter. August 2016.

Figure 148. The view towards Stourbridge includes the station buildings and the road over bridge behind. August 2016.

Hagley station is 140 miles and 29 chains (225.89km) from Paddington via Didcot, Oxford and Worcester.

Stourbridge Junction

Date Built	Railway/Design	Platforms	Passengers 2023–2024	Listed
1901 Rebuilt	Oxford, Worcester and Wolverhampton	3	1.261 million	No

Stourbridge Junction remains a junction, with the branch to Stourbridge Town at only 0.8 of a mile claiming to be the shortest in Europe. The station also had a large roundhouse-type engine shed until the 1960s, which had been full of pannier tanks, amongst other classes, to handle the multiplicity of trip and transfer freights from the numerous glassworks and collieries. Nowadays, north of Stourbridge Junction the main passenger line curves round to Birmingham Snow Hill and Moor Street with Chiltern Trains.

Figure 149. Stourbridge Junction station has been much modified and even moved in its lifespan. The third platform on the right is for the Stourbridge Town branch, and this is worked by two class 139 Parry People Mover units. December 2016.

Above: **Figure 150.** Stourbridge Junction Middle signal box no longer controls trains, and access to the town branch is controlled by the ground frame near the foot of the signal box steps. The two signs on the left prohibit class 139 units from passing that point, and the lower one advises that the limit of the One Train Staff train control has been reached. The Chiltern Rail depot has class 68 locomotives in attendance. December 2016.

Opposite above: **Figure 151.** As well as the Stourbridge Town branch to the left, the line splits after the depot for Walsall and Smethwick and Birmingham. December 2016.

Opposite below: **Figure 152.** Platform 3 has an array of seats—some GWR, some BR (WR)—and in the distance on the right, by the red signal light, is the class 139 depot. December 2016.

Stourbridge Junction station is 142 miles and 16 chains (228.85km) from Paddington via Didcot, Oxford and Worcester.

5

Gloucestershire

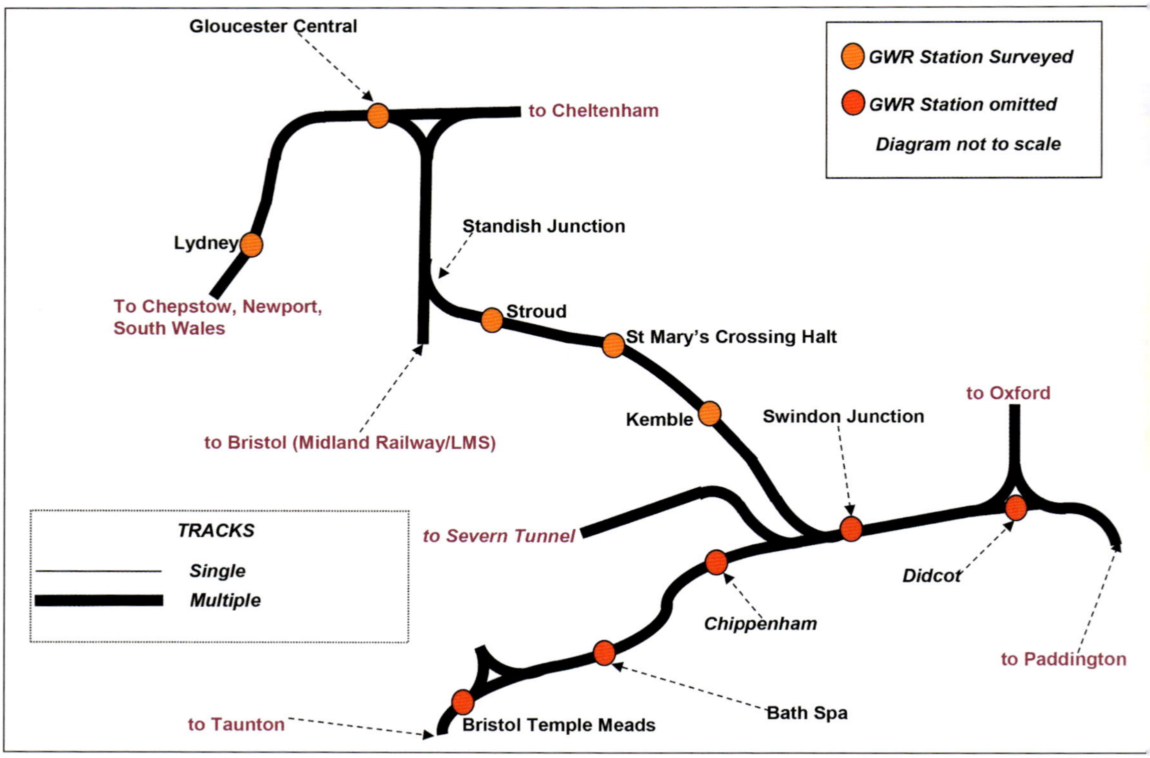

Figure 153. Gloucestershire—Kemble to Lydney. This journey takes in a way station for the Cheltenham Flyer express and humble coal trains from the Forest of Dean, although now in the past.

It is only recently that the Golden Valley main line from Swindon to Gloucester has been restored to full double track (Figure 153). This journey begins at Kemble.

Kemble

Date Built	Railway/Design	Platforms	Passengers 2023–2024	Listed
1882	GWR	2	0.400 million	Grade II

Kemble was another pre-Beeching double junction to Cirencester and Tetbury. Part of Cirencester station is now a Brunellian bus station, whilst some parts of Tetbury station and Culkerton goods shed survive in other use. Kemble is a fine station retaining many features, including the iconic water tower that provided Swindon with pumped drinking water.

Figure 154. Kemble station was an important junction of two branch lines, exemplified with this Cotswold stone frontage. The Cirencester branch platform was on the left and vestiges remain. The GWR pine trees provide an agreeable extra canopy. September 2016.

Figure 155. What late Victorian optimism inspired this light and airy hallway which leads to platform 1? It is now as busy with commuters at peak times as it was with the branch lines. The waiting room is comfortably furnished and has replica GWR posters on the walls. The 1934 Art Deco period cast iron seat mouldings look original, and the post box is late Georgian, so in-keeping. The station is the nearest for King Charles III's country home at Highgrove, but would originally have been Tetbury. September 2016.

Figure 156. Out on to the platform, and the decorative ironwork complements the stonework. The road over bridge is also listed and attributed to Brunel, built in 1840. The southward Kemble Tunnel (409yds/347m) was built to hide the railway from the view of a prominent local landowner as the price for granting GWR train passage. September 2014.

Figure 157. Class 150 DMU heads north out of platform 2 towards Stroud. The Tetbury branch platform was on the left side. September 2016.

Above: **Figure 158.** The view from the over bridge in Figure 156 looks south towards Swindon and the recently restored double track. The Cirencester platform curves away to the right and is now a siding for track maintenance vehicles. September 2016.

Right: **Figure 159.** The water tank is also listed and thought to date from 1882. There was originally a header tank above the main tank body, and the supporting iron bracketry can still be seen. September 2016.

Kemble station is 90 miles and 79 chains (146.43km) from Paddington via Swindon.

St Mary's Crossing Halt

Date Built	Railway/Design	Platforms	Passengers	Listed
1870s Signal box	GWR	Nil	Station closed	Grade II

The location between Chalford and Brimscombe was well known in steam days for trains banked up to the Sapperton Tunnels, and auto-trailers worked to Chalford from Gloucester. The signal box is the only structure hereabouts that remains of these workings other than the tunnels.

Figure 160. The halt of the same name disappeared in the 1960s, but the box was retained as a public crossing place for St Mary's Mill and some cottages. The signaller secures a gate at the request of a motorist and released by Gloucester Power Signal Box. February 2017.

St Mary's crossing is 98 miles and 64 chains (159km) from Paddington via Oxford.

Stroud

Date Built	Railway/Design	Platforms	Passengers 2023–2024	Listed
1845	Cheltenham and Great Western Union	2 (now in use)	0.583 million	Grade II

Stroud was an important mill town, prominent in wool processing, which was the generator of much wealth from the Middle Ages onwards. It is also the gateway to the beautiful Golden Valley, that gives access to Swindon and hence Paddington. The station is a major *tour de force* in stone, including the goods shed that retained its GWR painted lettering into this millennium. The footbridge, which is also Grade II listed, has recently been refurbished.

Figure 161. The class 43 HST makes a noisy departure for the short journey to Gloucester from Stroud station. The overgrown bay platform is for the Swindon direction. Note the bullhead rail used as platform edging. April 2016.

Figure 162. The main station building at Stroud is a rare Brunel original and even the modesty screen for the 'Gents' is built from Cotswold stone. April 2016.

Figure 163. The footbridge at Stroud is essentially complete and sports the intricate woodwork framing, as well as a complete top and sides. The Brunel goods shed with the grey doors is in the distance. April 2016.

Figure 164. A scene re-enacted many times over the years at Stroud, but now with a Paddington-bound HST instead of a Castle and ten coaches. The Golden Valley lies invitingly ahead. April 2016.

Figure 165. Brunel's GWR goods shed is looked after by a preservation society. The legend of the painted lettering is as follows:

GWR STROUD STATION GOODS TRAIN SERVICES
ONE DAY TRANSIT BETWEEN IMPORTANT TOWNS

April 2016.

Stroud station is 102 miles and 13 chains (164.41km) from Paddington via Swindon.

Gloucester Central

Date Built	Railway/Design	Platforms	Passengers 2023–2024	Listed
1914 Rebuilt	GWR	4	1.577 million	No

Cheltenham has seen its GWR stations closed en masse, whilst Gloucester's in the form of Central survived and Eastgate, Midland Railway, was closed. At Gloucester Central, even the vestiges of Horton Road steam sheds survive with even some diesels in attendance. The long through platform 1 at Gloucester could be divided into two, with a 'scissors' crossover and a banjo semaphore signal, as at Worcester Shrub Hill. Gloucester has a power signal box, which is also now under threat from Regional Control Centres.

Above: **Figure 166.** Gloucester station and the view here is of one of the longest platforms on the layout, divided into 1 and 2. The DMU in the distance is in platform 3, used for trains to South Wales. Note the class 31 on the right. March 2007.

Opposite above: **Figure 167.** Platform 3 is also known as the South Bay and alongside is the loading bay, known as Post Office Bank. FGW branded HST is in platform 2. Platform 3 had been the departure point for Gloucester to Hereford trains via Ross on Wye. March 2007.

Opposite below: **Figure 168.** What remains of Gloucester Horton Road steam depot (BR coded 85B) was home to a pair of Cotswold Rail class 47s, 47200 on the left. See the bullhead track and GWR manual point levers about the yard. March 2007.

Gloucester station is 114 miles and 4 chains (183.55km) from Paddington via Swindon.

Lydney

Date Built	Railway/Design	Platforms	Passengers 2023–2024	Listed
1918 Signal box	GWR	2	0.170 million	Signal box demolished

Lydney was the railhead and port for the Forest of Dean railways that were mainly concerned with colliery workings, and a connection exists for the heritage Dean Forest Railway. Now, only the Freeminers remain, granted an ancient right to dig their own coal if they satisfy certain residential qualifications. Lydney was also a port for canal and River Severn trade.

Figure 169. The only GWR structure left at Lydney station was this signal box, but this too succumbed in 2012. November 2003.

Figure 170. Lydney station goods loops just by the platforms, and it is from one of these that the connection is made to the Severn and Wye Railway, which is now the Dean Forest heritage line. This scene depicts a LM Region signal box (ex-Heysham) and Midland-esque paling fencing to underscore the joint GW and Midland nature of the Dean Forest line. The signal box also has a 'S&W' tag added on to Lydney Junction nameboard. November 2003.

Lydney station is 133 miles and 37 chains (214.79km) from Paddington via Swindon.

6

Severn Beach Line

This was a joint line, but between the Great Western and the Midland Railway (Figure 171). The line serviced commuters to Bristol as well as freight activities at Avonmouth Docks. This journey begins at Montpelier after departure from platform 1 at Bristol Temple Meads station.

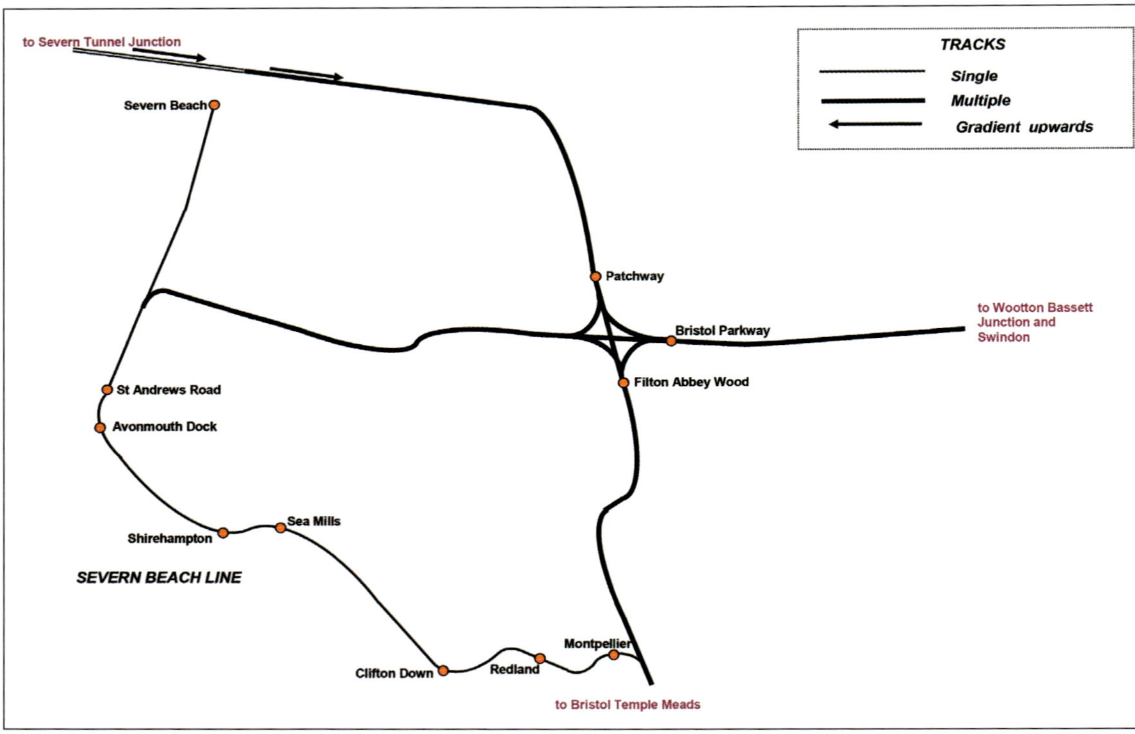

Figure 171. The Severn Beach Line.

Montpelier

Date Built	Railway/Design	Platforms	Passengers 2023–2024	Listed
1874	GWR/Midland	1	0.232 million	No

Montpelier is a suburb of Bristol and the station has reduced in size over the years like many others. The main reductions here, though, resulted from Luftwaffe raids in the Second World War. The tracks were reduced to a single line in 1970.

Figure 172. The line had originally been double track but was singled in the 1970s. Class 150, 150 127 is headed for Severn Beach after departure from Montpelier. Banksy is a Bristolian and some of the street art here perhaps has merit but is not his work. August 2016.

Montpelier station is 2 miles and 68 chains (4.59km) from Bristol Temple Meads station.

Redland

Date Built	Railway/Design	Platforms	Passengers 2023–2024	Listed
1897	GWR/Midland	1	0.211 million	Grade II footbridge

Redland station never had goods facilities, and so was always just a pure passenger commuter facility. The station building is as complete as any on the line and the footbridge is a joint railway oddity, neither markedly of GWR nor Midland origins.

Figure 173. Class 150, 150 938 draws to a stand at Redland station on its way to Bristol Temple Meads. The joint station building looks complete, framed by the listed footbridge which is distinctly un-GWR like. August 2016.

Redland station is 3 miles and 25 chains (5.33km) from Bristol Temple Meads station.

Clifton Down

Date Built	Railway/Design	Platforms	Passengers 2023–2024	Listed
1874	GWR/Midland	2	0.772 million	Grade II

Clifton Down is by far the most impressive station on the branch to service the upmarket district of Bristol. The station will forever be associated with Bristol Zoo, to which many excursions were run in steam days, often headed by Hall or Grange class 4-6-0 locomotives. In addition, the heavy routine GWR 1930s traffic was catered for by specially-built 'Clifton Down Auto Trailers', where two coach sets were used instead of the more usual one branch line coach, in which the locomotive operated in push-pull mode.

Figure 174. The magnificent station building and walls are listed at Clifton Down, despite the main building losing its canopies. There is a passing loop here. The bridge retains a whitewashed rectangle, used to make semaphore signal sighting easier. August 2016.

Clifton Down station is 3 miles and 72 chains (6.28km) from Bristol Temple Meads station.

Sea Mills

Date Built	Railway/Design	Platforms	Passengers 2023–2024	Listed
1906 Rebuilt	GWR/Midland	1	78,810	No

The station here never had a footbridge, but there was a subway which, alarmingly, would fill with water from the nearby river overflow. Passengers were then asked to cross the double track by a boarded rail crossing at the end of the platform.

Figure 175. Class 150, 150127 slows right down on the bridge over the River Trym, as Sea Mills station platform is off the end of the bridge. Thomas Cook, of the travel company, waxed lyrically on the scenic delights of the line. August 2016.

Figure 176. The Edwardian looking villa is Sea Mills station building, and the River Trym bridge was clearly double track. The vestiges of the other platform remain on the left. August 2016.

Sea Mills station is 6 miles (9.66km) from Bristol Temple Meads station.

Shirehampton

Date Built	Railway/Design	Platforms	Passengers 2023–2024	Listed
1865	Bristol Port and Pier	1	70,000	No

Shirehampton station had similar buildings to Redland, complete with a Midland Railway looking footbridge, but has not survived. Some work though has created small gardens bound by railway sleepers, anticipating the popular garden trend of using these substantial timbers by some years.

Figure 177. The original station buildings at Shirehampton were destroyed by fire in the 1990s. FGW branded class 150 DMU, 150938's passengers walk towards the exit. August 2016.

Shirehampton station is 7 miles and 50 chains (12.27km) from Bristol Temple Meads station.

Avonmouth

Date Built	Railway/Design	Platforms	Passengers 2023–2024	Listed
1885 Rebuilt	Bristol Port and Pier	2	0.13 million	No

Avonmouth docks helped pioneer the GWR importation of bananas from the West Indies which, in the 1930s, was an exotic and rare fruit. A Hall Class 4-6-0 would take a Cardiff-bound train of steam-heated, banana-covered fitted vans, tender first, down the branch to then connect with Pilning using the spur that existed then. At Pilning, the locomotive would run round and hence be the correct way for its onward journey. In more recent years, this millennium, Avonmouth Docks was a facilitator of imported coal for power station consumption, and one of its customers was Rugeley power station in Staffordshire.

Figure 178. The commodious shelter for dock workers going to work and returning home is still in place at Avonmouth, although the station building has gone. The platforms are now cut back from their original length and, as well as a passing loop, the near track is bi-directionally signalled. The dock workers' trains had been too long to be accommodated in the original platforms in 1955, where trains had to pull up twice. August 2016.

Avonmouth station is 9 miles and 2 chains (14.52km) from Bristol Temple Meads station.

St Andrews Road

Date Built	Railway/Design	Platforms	Passengers 2023–2024	Listed
1917	GWR and Midland	1	34,554	No

St Andrews Road is another station that serviced dock workers and the many industrial sites associated with the docks. Only one platform remains of the original station, which was advertised 'Only for Workmen's Trains' when opened in 1917, and closed in 1922. The station reopened in 1924 and ordinary passengers were then welcomed. The freight traffic that carries on leaves the Severn Beach line for a double-track branch line to Filton and Bristol Parkway (see Figure 171).

Figure 179. The signal box at St Andrews Junction controls the docks and industrial complex at Avonmouth. The mileage changes here, as denoted on the hefty concrete buffer stops and the mileage post, adds weight to the inscription. June 2016.

Figure 180. The coal hoppers for loading trains after transfer from ships are clearly on view, but now hardly used. Some DB Schencker Class 66 locomotives were stabled nearby and, although Britain still imports coal for the cement industry, the traffic is well down on what it was. The large vertical coal hopper was installed in 1993. Class 66 'bin liner' waste transfer trains are hauled nearby. August 2016.

The mileage changes here and is counted from a different direction. St Andrews Road station is 15 miles and 37 chains (24.88km) from Bristol Temple Meads station via the former Pilning Low Level station.

Severn Beach station has been reduced from a handsome terminus to a single platform and is about 4 miles (7km) further on.

Bibliography

Books and printed works

Clarke, R.H., and C.W. Judge, *An Historical Survey of Selected Great Western Stations: Volumes 1 to 4* (Headington: Oxford Publishing Company, 1976–1985)

Connelly, Philip, *British Railways Pre-Grouping Atlas and Gazetteer* (Shepperton: Ian Allan Publishing, 1976)

Cooke, R.A., *GWR Atlas of the Great Western Railway: 1947* (Didcot: Wild Swan Publications, 1988)

The Great Western Society Magazine

Kay, Peter, and Derek Coe, *Signalling Atlas and Signal Box Directory* (Stafford: Signalling Record Society, 2004)

Leigh, Chris, *Steam World* Magazine, Bauer Consumer Ltd., May 2025

Quail Track Diagrams: Parts 3&4, TrackMaps

Vaughan, Adrian, *Glory Days: Western Signalman* (Shepperton: Ian Allan Publishing, 2000)

Vaughan, Adrian, *Great Western Architecture* (Headington: Oxford Publishing Company, 1992)

Waters, Laurence, *Great Western: Halls and Modified Halls* (Barnsley: Pen & Sword Books Ltd., 2015)

Websites

Adrian the Rock's signalling pages: http://www.roscalen.com/signals

The Signalbox, John Hinson: www.signalbox.org/

Historic England: https://historicengland.org.uk/listing/the-list/

British Listed Buildings: http://www.britishlistedbuildings.co.uk/